Matija Mažuranić

A GLANCE
INTO OTTOMAN BOSNIA

or

A Short Journey into that Land
by a Native in 1839–40

[Published in Zagreb
at the expense of
the Royal Chartered Illyrian National Press
of Dr Ljudevit Gaj, 1842]

Translated by
Branka Magaš

SAQI
in association with
The Bosnian Institute

ISBN: 978-0-86356-830-5

This edition and translation © The Bosnian Institute (London), 2007

Originally published as *Pogled u Bosnu ili Kratak Put u onu Krajinu učinjen 1839–40. po Jednom Domorodcu*, in Zagreb at the expense of the Royal Chartered Illyrian National Press of Dr Ljudevit Gaj, 1842; second edition prepared in 1938 by Slavko Ježić, reprinted 1992 copyright © 1992, Konzor, Zagreb

This edition first published 2007

A full CIP record for this book is available from the British Library.
A full CIP record for this book is available from the Library of Congress.

Manufactured in Lebanon

SAQI

26 Westbourne Grove, London W2 5RH
825 Page Street, Suite 203, Berkeley, California 94710
Tabet Building, Mneimneh Street, Hamra, Beirut
www.saqibooks.com

in association with
The Bosnian Institute
14/16 St Mark's Road, London W11 1RQ
www.bosnia.org.uk

A GLANCE INTO OTTOMAN BOSNIA

Matija Mažuranić (1817–81) was the youngest brother of two leaders of the Illyrian national movement in Croatia, one of whom later became *ban* (viceroy) under Habsburg rule. Matija was to become an entrepreneur and builder of roads and bridges, who learned Turkish and travelled widely throughout the Ottoman Empire.

Branka Magaš is a native of Croatia living in London. The author of *The Destruction of Yugoslavia* (Verso) and *Croatia Through History* (Saqi), [and co-editor of *The War in Croatia and Bosnia-Herzegovina* (Frank Cass)], she is a consultant to The Bosnian Institute.

Contents

Introduction

Matija Mažuranić (1817–81) was born at Novi Vinodolski on the Croatian coast, in an area that by the end of the sixteenth century had become largely incorporated into the military border constructed against the Ottoman threat by Croatia's Habsburg kings. At the time of his birth, the border covered a large swathe of Croatian territory, starting at the Adriatic Sea and continuing eastwards along the River Sava (dividing Croatia from Bosnia) to the Danube, and beyond the Danube into Hungary. Croatia was then part of the Habsburg Monarchy, Bosnia and Serbia of the Ottoman Empire. The border marked the international frontier between the Monarchy and the Empire, but did not in fact wholly follow it, forming instead an elaborate pattern not unlike a clover leaf, its middle part cutting across to the River Drava approximately halfway between the Adriatic and what was then Croatia's easternmost town Zemun, located at the confluence of the Sava and the Danube opposite Belgrade. This configuration divided Croatia into the three disconnected segments of Dalmatia, Croatia and Slavonia.

The border was not simply a frontier area, but a complex military institution tightly run by the war office in Vienna, responsible only to the emperor-king. It was organised as eleven 'regiments', i.e. areas of population capable of raising one regiment each, within which all aspects of life were regulated by the military command and subordinated to its needs. The border behaved in many ways – and was indeed treated – like a separate province, albeit one devoid of any representative bodies. It contained the best roads and controlled the main navigable rivers. Although many of its officers and all its soldiers were native Croatians, the fact that it was run by the Austrians and its official language was German led it to be perceived as 'Germany' and its people as 'Germans'. The immediate neighbour of Bosnia and Serbia was thus 'Germany', not Croatia.

Matija was the youngest of five sons, two of whom – Antun and Ivan – played major roles in the Croatian *risorgimento* of the first half of the nineteenth century: Antun as a leading philologist, Ivan as a significant poet and later also ban (or regent, Croatia's highest political office-holder). At the time of Matija's journey to Bosnia, Antun and Ivan were living in Zagreb, seat of the national parliament, and were deeply involved in political and cultural activities aimed at turning Croatia into a modern nation. Matija's journey to Bosnia thus coincided with – and was indeed caused by – the arrival to political prominence of a new generation of leaders seeking to unify and modernise their country, and to make it into an independent state within the framework of the Habsburg Monarchy. One consequence of this design was a renewed interest in Bosnia, a country which, though a close neighbour, was practically unknown to most Croatians. This ignorance was due in large part to the existence of the military border, which prevented any easy communication between Croatia and Bosnia. You could legally cross into Bosnia only after first obtaining permission from the *Generalkomand*, which was no simple matter since the frontier with the Ottoman Empire was at all times closely guarded, and especially so in the 1830s. All cross-border traffic, in fact, took place under strict military supervision and at specially designated crossing points, of which there were two kinds. The larger ones, called *Contumaz Anstalten* or *kontumac*, served as quarantine stations for travellers and livestock. They were established at all major trading posts along the border with the Ottoman Empire, such as Kostajnica on the Una, Brod on the Sava, and Zemun. The smaller ones, which conducted more limited forms of disinfection, were called *Rastelle* or *raštel*. But there was also a lively contraband trade between Bosnia and Croatia, involving all sorts of goods and particularly salt.

The military border separated not only two empires – 'Austria' and 'Turkey' – but also two worlds, the West and the East, that were perceived largely in confessional terms: the West was Christian, the East Muslim. The gap between them was bridged, however, by a sense of the historical and cultural affinity of the lands and populations on its two sides. Educated Croatians had for some time been convinced, moreover, that all the South Slavs derived from ancient Illyrians, and were indeed prone to use 'Illyrian' as a synonym for 'South Slav'. This was particularly true for Mažuranić's generation who, preoccupied with the future of the South Slavs, came to be known as Illyrians. Since for them Croatia and Bosnia were parts of one and the same Illyrian land, the author – when setting off for Bosnia in late 1839 – felt that he was going not to a foreign land, but to a part of 'our Illyria', inhabited 'solely by our brothers, true Illyrians'.

What made Bosnia (with the newly created Herzegovina) particularly important in Croatian eyes was the fact that it was surrounded on two of its three sides (Mažuranić writes 'on all sides') by Croatia, and also that it included 'Turkish Croatia'. 'Turkish Croatia' denoted the area between the rivers Una and Vrbas in western Bosnia which Croatia had lost to the expanding Ottoman Empire. Its rivers and concurrent roads had formed traditional lines of trade and communication between Dalmatia and northern Croatia, and the loss of this territory was to cripple the Croatian state in this and the following century. Regaining 'Turkish Croatia' would mean bringing Dalmatia closer to Zagreb. Croatia's growing interest in Bosnia found eloquent expression in a brochure published in 1832 by the Croatian magnate and leading Illyrian politician Janko Drašković, in which he called for Croatia's political and economic regeneration on the basis of the creation – nominally within the Habsburg Monarchy – of a 'Kingdom of Illyria' that would include, in addition to a united Croatia, most of present-day Slovenia and all of Bosnia-Herzegovina.

Such grand visions were encouraged by great changes then occurring in Europe, especially in the Ottoman Empire. In 1830 the Serb 'Illyrians' of the new principality of Serbia won autonomy for themselves, after which the Ottoman – and Muslim – presence there was reduced to six frontier garrisons. The Muslim landowners lost their property and were forced to leave, with many ending up in Bosnia, where they continued to dream of returning one day in force. Bosnia, on the other hand, spent much of the 1830s in a state of intermittent civil war. It was run at the time by a small group of begs centred on Sarajevo, sufficiently powerful to force the imperial representative (vizier) to remove himself to Travnik. In 1831 the begs rose against the Porte (the Ottoman court at Constantinople), partly in protest at having to surrender some of the territory of the Bosnian or Sarajevo pashalik to Serbian jurisdiction, and demanded autonomy for Bosnia too. Their revolt was crushed in the following year with the aid of the Muslim notables of Herzegovina, which explains flashes of anti-Herzegovina anger registered by Mažuranić in this book. Then, in 1834 and 1835, there were uprisings of Christian peasantry in several parts of Bosnia. In 1835 the imperial government, determined to reinforce its control, abolished the peculiarly Bosnian system of kapetans underpinning the power of the local Muslim landlords, and replaced it with a government run by imperial officials. Some of the kapetans in western Bosnia took to arms; but they were defeated with the support of the border army, since Vienna regularly sided with the sultan. There was another, equally unsuccessful revolt of Bosnian notables in 1837. In late 1839 (i.e. at the time when Mažuranić set off for Bosnia) Istanbul initiated a fresh wave of reforms that was equally unwelcome to the Bosnian Muslim elite. As Mažuranić was able to discover on his arrival, Bosnia was by now in pretty poor shape, given that neither the central state nor the local ruling class was able to establish fully its authority over the country.

Drašković's list of peoples inhabiting his projected Kingdom of Illyria excluded (for unspecified reasons) the Bosnian

Muslims, whom he called Turks – and who indeed, according to Mažuranić, themselves insisted on being called Turks. It was nevertheless in order to ascertain the national sentiments of these 'Illyrian Turks' rebelling against the Porte that Matija was sent on a secret mission to Bosnia by his brothers Antun and Ivan (acting undoubtedly on behalf of their Illyrian circle gathered around Drašković), who apparently hoped that the Bosnian Muslims' struggle might result in Bosnia's liberation from Ottoman rule. An Ottoman departure from Bosnia would make the military border wholly redundant, thus freeing Croatia from the Austrian military presence on its soil. Such developments would in turn create conditions for the eventual union of the Croatian and Bosnian parts of 'Illyria'.

This background explains why Mažuranić's book concentrates almost exclusively upon the Muslim – indeed the urban Muslim – component of Bosnia: its language and material culture, its social and sexual mores, its religious practices and superstitions, the position of its women, the mentality and forms of domination of its leaders, the discrimination against the Christian population – which inevitably extended to him as well. He also registers its aspirations and fears – and its growing resignation. Mažuranić is not a disinterested commentator, given the nature of his mission; but he is a level-headed observer, inspired by curiosity rather than prejudice. At the same time, he was only twenty-two years old when he went to Bosnia and could not but feel deeply humiliated by the ridicule inspired by his dress, his confession and his manners.

A Glance into Ottoman Bosnia is fascinating not only in what it tells us about contemporary Bosnia, but also because it gives an insight into the main problem faced by the ideologues of 'Illyria': how to conceive the unity of its parts, given such diversity of its polities. A most illuminating exchange in this regard between Mažuranić and his Bosnian audience concerned the presence of Turkish, or Ottoman, words in the local language. The Illyrians at the time were busily removing German, Italian and Hungarian words and constructions from the Croat language, a task they saw as a *sine qua non* of their country's political emancipation. When Mažuranić tried to explain to the Bosnians that they too should give up 'foreign' words as being alien to their language, the Bosnians staunchly defended them, arguing that they were not alien at all, but had in fact been borrowed by the Turks from Bosnian! Mažuranić, in their view, simply did not know Bosnian, which was not quite true. On the other hand, he did learn Turkish, unlike many of the Bosnian pashas.

On his return to Zagreb in 1841, Matija submitted a written report to the effect that, while the leading Bosnian begs were in their hearts nationally minded and desirous of freedom, their movement was weak, because it was more narrowly Muslim than national in character. The population itself had not as yet been 'awakened', but the conditions of its life were such that it might rise up at any time. After stripping the text of Matija's report of anything that might be politically embarrassing, his brothers had it published in 1842 as a travelogue. The Illyrians' sympathetic interest in Muslim Bosnia was to continue thereafter, giving rise to important literary works on the part of Matija's brother Ivan: *The Death of Smail-Aga Čengić*, and the cantos completing Ivan Gundulić's great epic poem *Osman*, were written and published between 1842 and 1846.

Matija Mažuranić's book consists of three parts. The first, 'To Bosnia and Back', describes his journey to Bosnia, his life in Sarajevo and the return journey to Croatia. The second, 'Diverse Observations on Bosnia', is more anthropological in nature and concerns the way of life of the Bosnian Muslims. The third is a brief glossary of 'Turkish Barbarisms'. In 1964, when the book was republished, a short postscript by the Croatian literary historian Antun Barac was added, which is also reproduced here. In order to help the reader track Matija's journey, a brief summary of his itinerary follows.

Croatia: 31 October–14 November 1839
Karlovac–Glina–Sisak–Jasenovac–Kostajnica–Dubica
Mažuranić's initial plan was to walk from Karlovac to Sisak and thence on to Kostajnica; but when after some trouble he did manage to reach Kostajnica, he found that the military authorities would not let him cross into Bosnia without an international passport. He did nevertheless succeed in getting into Bosnia by illegally crossing the River Sava at Dubica; but once there he chose to turn back, when it became clear that the local official was not able to procure him a pass to Sarajevo.

Croatia: 14–24 November 1839
Dubica–Jasenovac–Zemun–Pančevo–Zemun
Foiled at this end of the border, he decided to enter Bosnia by way of Serbia. Having failed to find a boat at Jasenovac that would take him down the Sava to Zemun, he instead made his

way by land. Once in Zemun, he made another illegal crossing, this time to Belgrade.

Serbia: 25 November–5 December 1839
Belgrade–Grocka–Smederevo–Palanka–Kragujevac–Čačak–Požega–Užice–Mokra Gora
The transit through Serbia was the easy part of Matija's journey. Turning right at Belgrade, he proceeded along the Danube to Smederevo, and from there down the valley of the River Morava to Kragujevac, where he turned right again to Čačak and, continuing in the same direction, reached the Serbian-Bosnian border post at Mokra Gora.

Bosnia: 5 December–11 December 1839
Višegrad–Sarajevo
The first port of call on the Bosnian side was Višegrad, whence – crossing 'those forbidding mountains' – he made his way to Sarajevo. Immediately upon his arrival he joined the retinue of the pasha of Sarajevo.

Bosnia: 18 December–29 December 1839
Sarajevo–Visoko–Travnik
Following upon the vizier's order that all Bosnian pashas should meet him in Travnik, Matija accompanied his own on a journey of two days, riding 'Tartar-style'. He celebrated Christmas in Travnik.

Bosnia: 30 December 1839–19 January 1840
Travnik–Busovača–Rakovica–Sarajevo
News of an uprising in Sarajevo caused his pasha to turn back. Due to the hardship of travel in a bitterly cold winter, Matija fell ill with fever. He left the pasha's service. Acting under pressure, he decided to leave Bosnia and return home by way of Serbia.

Bosnia: 19 January–27 January 1840
Sarajevo–Brezovača–Mokro–Hanić–Nova Kasaba–Kuzlar–Zvornik
Matija survived this journey thanks to the kindness of the Orthodox and Muslim people he met while travelling or resting.

Serbia: 27 January–6 February 1840
Rača–Šabac–Palež Obrenovac–Belgrade
Once again the journey through Serbia was trouble-free, although Matija continued to suffer from fever. Lack of money then led him to spend ten months in Belgrade working as an apprentice.

Croatia: 13 December 1840–7 January 1841
Zemun–Vukovar–Osijek–Bjelovar–Zagreb
Back in Croatia, Matija was promptly arrested for crossing illegally into Serbia, and expelled under guard from the military border. He journeyed along Croatia's northern rim back to Zagreb.

Branka Magaš

Note on this Edition

All the footnotes are Mažuranić's own, as are the glossary and its definitions. The author's renderings and Croatian transliterations of Turkish words, the meanings he gives for the latter, his Croatised Turkish morphemes and his grammatical glosses remain as in the original (no exception being made even for inconsistencies, irregularities or errors). A translation has been provided in the text here, between square brackets, of words of Turkish (or Arabic, Persian, etc.) origin that Mažuranić did not include in his glossary, seeing no need to elucidate them since they were already current in the Croat language at the time when he was writing.

A Glance into Ottoman Bosnia

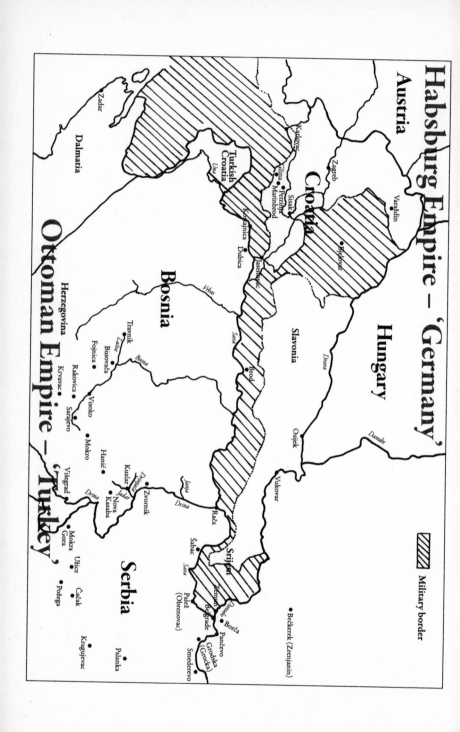

Preface

*B*osnia, this neighbouring Turkish province, with the associated Herzegovina and Turkish Croatia, is surrounded on all sides by Austrian lands, i.e. by Croatia, Slavonia and Dalmatia. The Turkish border at its nearest point is not much further from Zagreb than Bjelovar and only a little further than Varaždin, i.e. around eleven miles, while along the mail road through Petrinja there are not more than twelve miles to the Kostajnica *raštel* [see Introduction]. To the inhabitants of Karlovac, the Turkish border is closer than Zagreb. Not only are the Turks our nearest neighbours, but also nearly one-third of our small kingdom of Croatia, i.e. the whole of the area between the Una and the Vrbas, is ruled by the Turks. Notwithstanding this, however, there are few of our educated countrymen who would not be able to tell you more about America, China, India, etc. than about Bosnia. The reason for this is not difficult to fathom.

During more than 200 years our ancestors invested a good deal of effort and shed much blood fighting the Turks. However, for some eighty or ninety years (thanks to divine providence and the endeavours of a beneficent government) since a military border was established alongside Turkey and a strong guard placed on the frontier, we have enjoyed a respite from this great toil, so that feeling secure from that side we have turned our back on it in order to find out what was happening in the cultured West. It seems that we have not turned round since that time. Continuing to look westwards, we have come to know the Germans and the Italians, the French and the English, better than ourselves. As for the rest of the world, we know no more than what we have managed to learn from our nearest western neighbours, who naturally know next to nothing about Bosnia either.

But must it always be like this? Is it not time for us to finally turn round and find out for ourselves in the most direct way about the conditions prevailing in this part of our Illyria?

It was these and similar thoughts which awoke in me the desire, having travelled as a journeyman (*kalfa*) through the greater part of the Austrian Empire, and especially all its Illyrian lands, to acquaint myself better with Bosnia too. But how? There are no books, and I had never met a traveller who went there with the sole purpose of learning about the land, its language and customs. I therefore decided that, come what may, I myself should travel to the Bosnian province. I offer here to the kind reader the knowledge and experience I acquired there as faithfully as my pen allows. It is true that none of us is likely to come to know this country well from here; but I nevertheless believe that those of my countrymen who enjoy reading such reports about different states in the world will be glad to learn, at their ease and in the safety and comfort of their homes, at least as much about this neighbouring land (inhabited, moreover, solely by our own Illyrian kin) as I have done, exposed to mortal danger, during my stay there. It was my intention to remain there even longer, and to explore the whole country in all the year's seasons, but my failing health forced me to cut my journey short.

The Author

Part I

To Bosnia and Back

I arrived in Karlovac on 31 October [1839]. I sought to go by boat to Jasenovac, but at that time the boats were still moving up the Kupa, so I decided to proceed on foot to Sisak. I spent three days in Karlovac. I was advised there that by taking a route other than the main road I would shorten by several stages my journey to Sisak. On arriving at the village of Toran I was to turn left and then follow the path from village to village as far as Petrinja.

I left Karlovac on 3 November. I turned left at Toran, came to a village, and asked for a short cut to Sisak. No one there knew what Sisak was, however, or in what part of the world it might lie. But now that I had come this way, they said, I should proceed to another village, where someone might possibly know the way to this Sisak of mine. I struck out along the route they showed me and, often coming to some crossroads or other and having no one to ask, I would follow what seemed to me to be the most frequented path, thinking it must needs be the main road.

Following this route I found myself in the midst of a forest, where paths branched out in all directions and the main road disappeared. I had eaten nothing the whole day, apart from a morning shot of *rakia* [grape brandy] in Karlovac, not having taken so much as a bread roll with me. The sun in the sky had been hidden the whole day long, and it seemed to me that it was growing dark. I hurried along the path that appeared most direct, but by the time I reached its end I was in complete darkness. Whither now, I wondered, without a road, at night? There was plenty of wood around, but since I unfortunately do not smoke a pipe, I had no tinderbox with me with which to light a fire somewhere where I could spend the night. I told myself I should have to walk the whole night, no matter in which direction; for in the first place it was possible that I might come across a village, and secondly I should avoid catching cold sitting somewhere throughout the long winter night without a fire.

Wandering in this manner I came to a knoll whence I discerned a fire in the distance, which suddenly vanished. I stopped to look: the fire shone forth three or four times, only to as quickly disappear. It occurred to me that this must be a house, with its door towards me: its inhabitants were not asleep but were moving in and out through the door, which would account for the fire's intermittent appearance. I made directly for the place over all sorts of hollows and ditches, somehow managed to find a path, and – taking care not to lose it in the dark – arrived at a house. Its inhabitants, who were still awake, opened the door to me and cheerfully offered to put me up. The house was the home of two married brothers, both still young and childless. The little they had in the house was clean and beautifully tidy, and all four of them were nicely and cleanly dressed. They treated me to a neat if rustic supper, accompanied by plenty of wine. We roasted corn[1] and potatoes, cracked walnuts, and moistened our throats with wine. We talked for a long while, after which the wives made me a bed of straw, which they covered with two sheets and a blanket, placing a pillow at the head.

When we arose in the morning they showed me the way and I set off. But to no avail: with the roads crossing each other everywhere, I knew not how to proceed. So I did as before, keeping to larger roads, and met the same fate once again – ending up in the woods as on the previous day. Thanks to the heavy rain that had fallen during these first days, there was mud and puddles everywhere. I came to a broad old oak, under which shepherds must have lit fires, since the flames had carved out a kind of hollow where one could shelter from the rain, while two logs lay beside the hearth where the shepherds used to sit. By now I had my fill of struggling through the muddy forest, so I sat there for a moment to rest awhile. I took off the bag from my back and began to reflect deeply on how I should proceed next time in the matter of shortcuts.

Once I had rested and committed the rule to memory, I picked up my bag and carried on. With cloudy skies hiding the sun, I had no way of telling whether I was going east or west, as though it were night. My sole concern was to avoid breaking my neck. At times I followed a road, at others a path, depending on where the way led me. After walking for a good four hours, I found myself at the very oak tree under which I had earlier rested. Not believing my own eyes, I looked around, but all looked the same as it had been that afternoon and it was impossible to mistake

---

1. After harvesting the maize they place it in a cave or cellar, so that they have something to roast throughout the autumn.

the tracks of my boots at the place where I had sat. So on this spot I had another stab at memorising the rule about using short cuts in future. I told myself that I could spend a week in this manner, circling around one and the same forest without ever reaching a village. Seeing that night was falling, however, I hurried off in another direction, where so far as I could tell the path was becoming better and wider. But by this time it had grown quite dark. Until now I had moved to whichever side of the road was less muddy, but it was now necessary to keep to the middle even if this meant having mud up to my neck. During the night I came to a house containing more occupants, albeit poorer than those at my previous lodging; but they nevertheless received me gladly and regaled me as well as they could. They told me that I would not hereafter get lost again, but would follow a proper road from village to village and at lunchtime arrive at Glina. Otherwise, if I took a short cut, it would take me more than two weeks to reach Sisak. I rose early the following morning and arrived in Glina in time for lunch, went from Glina to Marinbrod for the night, and from there went with a coachman to Sisak on 6 November 1839.

I spent two days at Sisak. On 9 November I sailed with the Zemun *burćela*[1] downstream to Jasenovac. Once there I decided to walk along the Una to Kostajnica, where, if they would let me, I could cross into Bosnia. Back home I had decided against taking out a passport to leave the realm, not wishing people to know where I was heading. But it was impossible to obtain a passport from the *Generalkomand* for anything but a short period, which was of no use to me so I did not bother to apply.

---

1. A *burćela* is a small boat.

I thought that if they would not let me across the bridge at Kostajnica, I would smuggle myself across the Una. On arriving in Kostajnica I went to the Border command, but in vain: they told me they could not let me cross the bridge without a full passport. I then secretly questioned the local people about how to cross over undetected. They advised me that this could best be done downstream at Dubica, where contraband from Turkey passed as well. I consequently turned back towards Dubica, and arriving at the crossing point I saw a well-dressed young gentleman carrying a leather bag slung across one shoulder, who kept glancing towards the Turkish side. When he saw me he pretended not to be concerned and quickly approached me. We exchanged greetings and asked one another whence we came. Since I had already guessed his intentions, I was the first to disclose that I wished, if possible, to go to Turkey. He said that this was his intention too; that he wished to go by way of Bosnia to Serbia, where he would become a priest, since times were hard; and that he was highly educated and could sing beautifully in church, and that once in Serbia he might easily become a bishop. I asked him where he had been born and how he made his living. He told me he had been born in Brod in Slavonia; and moreover that he was a teacher, who travelled around in this way and whenever the opportunity arose to teach anybody anything and so earned his living. I thought to myself: you think you have found a fool you can cheat, but you can tell that story to someone else. But for the sake of his company through Turkey, which would make things more pleasant, I preferred not to harbour bad thoughts about him. So we agreed on how to get across, and what to say to the Turks when we met them. Consequently we walked to the river bank, some 50 ells from the road, and sat under a willow. My teacher then whistled through his fingers in the *hajduk* [brigand] manner and waved his arm, upon which the Turks[1] jumped into a punt and came across. They approached us and asked us what we wanted. We said we were eager to enter Turkey to work as craftsmen, since there were too many masters in Germany, which made life hard. They told us they could take us over cheaply, but did not know what the *spahija* would say. We told them we should easily deal with the *spahija*; all they had to do was take us across. The Turk said: '*Valaha*, I shall take you over; give me twenty kreutzers apiece and you can go all the way to stone-built Zadar, if you please.' We promptly jumped into the boat and they drew away.

The river at this point is very broad but shallow, which is why no oars are needed and you propel yourself by means of poles. The water is shallowest in the middle, and there we got stuck. While the Turks were pushing the boat a little farther upstream, where it was deeper, some shepherds showed up on the German side and, seeing a Turkish boat with two men dressed in the German style, began to shout at the tops of their voices: 'Two men have escaped! Two men have escaped!' The Turks hastened to relaunch the boat, and after getting across led us into their hut, after which the shepherds on the other side finally stopped shouting. The Turks sent their Vlach[2] to fetch the *spahija*, and it was only then that the two of us began to feel frightened. Although we tried to hide it, this was of no avail since we started

---

1. One of them was a Turk, the other a Christian. Our people call all people from the Turkish land 'Turks', just as the Turks call all German subjects 'Swabians' (*Švabe*).

2. The Turks call Illyrians of the Greek and Roman confessions 'Vlachs'.

to tremble like leaves. We talked to each other in German about how to face the *spahija,* who might turn out to be an unkind man; he could even take us in bonds to Kostajnica and hand us over to the *Švabe* [Swabians, i.e. Germans]. At this point another Turk arrived, a big barefooted man wearing tattered *dimije* [baggy trousers][1] although it was winter, a threadbare *anteria* [embroidered wide-sleeved tunic], a soiled *jelek* [embroidered sleeveless jacket] and a *ćurak* [sheepskin coat] with all its hems torn and hanging down. There was a *čalma* [turban] on his head, somewhat below that a sparse beard, and a *čibuk* [pipe] in his hand made from a hollowed out walnut shoot. He sat down on his heels[2] beside the wooden bridge, then, alternately adjusting the *čalma* with his hands and stroking his sparse beard and whiskers, he started to converse with us.

Waiting as we were for the *spahija* we had no desire to talk to anyone else, and told the Turk we were waiting for the *spahija*. He replied that he was the *spahija*, which is why he had come. We quickly glanced at one another and apologised to the *spahija*, asking him to forgive us for not doing him the honours, but we had not known who he was. He bid us not to worry, since in any case it was not their custom to do honours to individuals as was habitual in Germany; and said that we should merely tell him why we had come and what we wanted. We replied that we were artisans, and that it was no longer possible to make a living in Germany because of its multitude of masters, which is

1. *Dimije* are worn only in summer. They are made of white or multicoloured cotton. *Dimije* are also worn by women.

2. The Turks like to sit cross-legged when they are not walking. In places that are muddy and dirty, they simply squat on their heels. They can squat and converse like that all day long.

why we wished to go to glorious Turkey and there practise our craft. He said that he would have let us in, had the shepherds on the other side not seen us. 'But the *Švabe*' – he said – 'are evil people who will write to their general. The general will protest to the *kadia* [judge] in Dubica, and the *kadia* will then ask me questions. I might simply tell him that some people came to buy salt and returned back the same night, but I could not take upon myself this worry for nothing, so you should pay me something.' We replied that we were poor men who had nothing; if we had money, we would have remained at home rather than having to endure the hardship of travelling around. '*Valaha*, I know', he said, 'that a warm cake drives no one from home; but let me have at least your pocket watches and tents.[1] I myself do not in fact need such things,' he continued, 'but I would make a present of one to the *ajan* and the other to the *kadia*; after which you will be able to go where you wish all over Turkey.' We looked at each other and asked the *spahia* whether he could supply us with a document, so that we would not be stopped elsewhere. '*Valaha*, I would give it to you, if only I could write; but I swear by my *din* that you will not need it. Ten years ago I myself went to Sarajevo and, by *aman*,[2] no one asked me for a document.'

This appeared to us too costly; we would, moreover, not be safe without such a document. So we requested that they transport us back; if it proved possible, we would come again

---

1. He did not know the word for umbrellas, so called them tents; yet I did hear people in Bosnia speak of umbrellas.

2. I do not know what *aman* means in Turkish, but Bosniaks use it for naming many things, such as 1. faith; 2. baths; 3. when one is beaten on the soles of his feet he shouts *aman*; 4. *amanet* or pledge; 5. when one sings he ends each line with *aman, aman*. *Din* or 'by my *din*' means 'by my faith' or 'I swear'.

another time. 'Fine, fine,' said the *spahia*, 'you can come at night too; go then, lads, take them back to the other side.' The two who had brought us and to whom I had earlier given two twenties – since my teacher had asked me to pay for him too, because he had no small change: we should easily settle this later – jumped up. We thus returned to the German side without anyone noticing us, and reached the first inn along the way at about two o'clock in the afternoon of 14 November.

Here we lunched together; but when it was necessary to pay it turned out that my teacher had not a single kreutzer in his pocket. This made me angry: why did he tell me in the morning that he lacked small change, when now he has neither small sums nor large? I forced him to show me his passport, so that I might see who he was and whence he came. However, he drew from his breast a furrier's *Wanderbuch*, saying that he was both a teacher and a *ćurčia* [fleece-maker]. I thought to myself that he deserved to be cursed at; but that if he were shameless this would be to no avail; if, on the other hand, he was a minimally honest pauper, it would suffice that his lies had been laid bare. I therefore paid the innkeeper the whole bill, fully convinced by now that he must indeed be a teacher, since he had taught me a lesson about keeping company with strangers. I then set off for Dubica on my way to Jasenovac, where I spent the night. Since I failed to catch a boat there, I travelled by land across Slavonia, sometimes by coach and sometimes on foot, and arrived in Zemun on 20 November.

From Zemun Belgrade seemed far away, across a watery crossroads that looked like an open sea. I set off in a wooden boat (made of deal planks) for Pančevo, thinking that this would be a good place to cross the Danube. The Danube is indeed narrow at Borča, but at Pančevo it grows vastly broad again. Luckily the Pančevo merchants had no wheat, so my wooden boat returned along the Danube in the direction of Bečkerek and took me on to Zemun. I asked a fisherman in Zemun whether he could take me across to Belgrade. He asked how many of us there were. 'Just me,' I replied. 'Bah, it wouldn't do for a single person unless he was rich, since no one would risk his skin for less than fifty silver francs.'

I had parted from the fisherman when a master-craftsman approached me saying: 'My friend, you wish to go to Belgrade?' 'Who told you?' I asked. 'You don't need to be secretive in front of me,' he said, 'because I won't press you. I only heard you talk about it with the fisherman. The fisherman can't do it without good pay, because many have already been punished for it. But I can tell you what you should do. I have a *čun* [dinghy] which I no longer need. If you give me what I paid for it, I'll give you an oar and, if you know how to navigate, you can go to Belgrade by yourself.' He then showed me the boat and where his house was; if I wished, we could go to his place and talk about it. I first had lunch, and then went to see him. He told me that the boat cost only 2 silver francs, and that I could bring my things to his place and even sleep there. He would wake me up the next day, hand me the oar, and let me go with the Lord's blessing. This is indeed what happened: he woke me at four o'clock in the morning, and gave me an oar and a clay bowl (*činia*). He strongly advised me not to go along the great Danube, because an Austrian *šajka* was anchored off Belgrade keeping watch by night for people wishing to cross in either direction. I should also avoid setting off from the Banat side, since the guards might spot me from their watchtower. I should navigate instead through the small islets (*adice*) until I reached the sands of Dorćul beneath Belgrade. After he gave me all this information, I thanked him warmly and, having taken my things, made for the water. Pushing the boat into the water, I placed my bag in it, sat myself down in it too, and started to paddle. The boat must have spent some time on land, since it promptly began to leak. I was alternately paddling and scooping out water when suddenly a fog descended, and there was nothing to be seen but the water on which I was navigating. An evil wind started to blow too, and waves began to heave on the water as if it were a sea. My craft, already weak, was taking water through its bottom in the same measure as the waves were filling it from above. Letting go of the oar, I took the bowl in both hands and started to bale the water out of the boat, but to my great distress a single wave would bring in more water than I could cast out in ten strokes. I began to doubt that I would be able to save myself that morning. If it were summer, I said to myself, I would not worry, because I am a good swimmer; but if I founder now I shall perish from the cold. And when I die and the water delivers me onto some shore, the people who find me will never know who I am or whence I come. So I quickly took my passport from my bag and put it in my pocket, thinking that when the people discovered me they would dry my passport and find out. At the same time I also took out the money from my bag and tucked the pouch into my bosom, after which I buttoned myself up tightly so that it would not fall out into the water: let this too be found on me. I felt semi-conscious – I knew not which way from me lay

Zemun nor how to get to Belgrade. I could not put my hand into the water to feel the flow of the current because of the waves, and the wind, moreover, was blowing from all sides like a northeaster [*bura*]. Luckily this was the time of the Turkish *Ramazan,* so the *hodže* [imams] got up early that morning to light lanterns on the minarets, and the wind also began to whip up the waves a little less. I was able, therefore, after emptying the water from the boat, to paddle for as much as an hour in the direction of Belgrade's lights. I managed to squeeze myself in between the little islets (although I did not even see them that morning), and arrived at Dorćul beneath Belgrade on 25 November just as dawn broke.

I pulled my boat onto the land alone, then went to see Master Kosta, a fisherman and butcher. I sat with him until eight o'clock, after which he took me to the magistrate's court. I was well received there, especially by the head of the magistrate's court: he told the other gentlemen about it, and they were all glad that I had had such a lucky escape. I requested they enter into my passport permission to visit Smederevo, which they promptly did. I went by way of Grodska and arrived in Smederevo on 28 November.

Of all the Serbian towns which I subsequently saw, I liked Smederevo least. The town is laid out on a plain alongside the Danube, I would say in a kind of hollow. At that time the mud in it reached the ankle, while one could not hug the walls for fear of bumping one's head against the eaves of the houses. I took a brief walk to see the fort. It is situated on a modest elevation and surrounded by a very high wall with small square bastions built into it, separated some 15 ells one from another and somewhat taller than it. Outside the wall a shallow entrenchment of evidently more recent date has been made for guns; it is amateurishly constructed in comparison with the great wall. Several Turkish guns were in evidence, with oaken platforms beneath them and wheels of a kind that looked like millstones, but it had all rotted away beyond repair, and some guns had already toppled over onto the ground. I walked through the gate into the fort, to a Turkish coffee house where guards sit barring the way beyond. Inside I sat on a *divanhana*,[1] drank a coffee and looked beyond into the fort. One could see nothing save a few Turkish huts made of wattle and plastered with dung, not as good as the kind made by our herdsmen in the forest when guarding cattle in summertime. I asked the Turks why one was not free to walk around the fort. It is forbidden, they replied, not just to you but to all, Turks included, who have no business there. One whispered to me that it was on account of the women. I went on to my *mehana* and on the way had my passport for Kragujevac signed at the magistrate's court. In the evening citizens of Smederevo – both Serbs and Turks – came to the inn where I was staying, some to drink wine, others coffee.[2] They asked me whence I came. When I told them, one old Turk stroked his beard and began a tale.

Once, before the start of Kara-Đorđe's war, the local people grew restless, for which the Turks laid the blame on our Smederevo

---

1. A *divanhana* is a kind of enclosed gallery to be found in all the better houses, coffee houses and inns. Here the Turks sit in the summer, smoke and converse.

2. *Kafana* and *mehana* are practically the same, the difference being that a *kafana* does not have a courtyard for visitors, while every *mehana* contains a room called the *Kafana*.

kadia and decided to execute him. When he learned of this, the poor man fled across Šumadia and Bosnia straight to Trieste, where he planned to sail with merchants on a *galia*[1] to Istanbul, there to clear his name. On arriving in Trieste he left his baggage at an inn and took a walk through the town to look at the infidels' strange buildings. Wherever he looked he could see that streets and squares had beautiful, clean pavements made of marble;[2] that the outsides of the houses, rising up to the clouds, were embellished with all manner of attractive decorations; and that at ground level were to be found wonderful shops full of all kinds of goods and crafts. He came, *efendum benum* (dear Sir), to a street where he met two beautiful girls, tall and slender like two pines. As they came up to him, they suddenly grabbed him by his beard and whiskers with the intention of wrenching them off. The poor man tried to defend himself, but there were two of them, and he found it impossible to escape. Luckily an infidel came by who had travelled many times to Istanbul on business and was thus able to speak Turkish. He managed to fend them off, and told him in Turkish that the sight of a beard and whiskers made their girls particularly angry; if he wished to be left in peace, he should go to a barber and have them taken off. Otherwise their girls would tear out all his nails. The poor man fled to his inn, which he henceforth feared to leave. The innkeeper, however, was a kind man, who went every day to the quay to look out for a boat being readied for Istanbul. He found him a boat and accompanied him through the town – so that the girls would not harm him – all the way to the boat. Once in

---

1. By *galia* they mean a sea boat.
2. Serbs and Bosniaks call all hard stone marble.

Istanbul he managed to clear his name before the Grand Vizier, and having returned once again to be *kadia* here in Smederevo, told us what had happened to him on his journey.

While the ancient was telling this story, the young Turks were smoking their *čibuki* [chibouks][1] and hanging on to his every word. When the old man ended, the Turks one and all started to give me hostile looks, thinking how I was here with them in peace, while in my country their *kadia* had suffered so much evil.[2]

On the morning of 29 November I travelled to Palanka, where I put up for the night. I rose early on the following morning and, because it was rather cold, I took leather gloves out of my pocket and put them on, thinking that I would thus be more comfortable. When coming out of the town, I took a wrong turning. After going on for a long time I met a farmer riding a horse, and asked him whether this was the way to Kragujevac. 'Well,' he said, 'it is not. You have missed the road by far. You should turn round, and I will tell you the way.' Having said this, he grew scared and descended into deep silence. Whenever I asked him something, he refused to say a word. I saw that something was upsetting him, and wishing to cheer him up started to talk of this and that. After continuing together for a long time, he realised that I was a man not some supernatural being and became bold enough to ask me: 'Listen, my lad, can you tell me what you have there – why are your hands so black?

1. *Čibuk* means the stem of the pipe, but the stem and the pipe together are also called *čibuk*. They would be greatly offended if someone asked them to pass on the pipe as opposed to the chibouk.

2. The Turks still think that Šumadia (which is how they maliciously call Serbia) belongs to them; that dear Allah has only been punishing them for their sins, and that they will once again be masters there.

You have no nails or anything, and your skin is full of folds.' So that was it! I took my gloves off and showed him that it was not my skin, but only gloves.[1] He began to cross himself with both his left hand and his right, saying: 'There, I have spent so much time in trade and in the army without ever seeing such devilry. See what kind of things are made abroad, whereas we over here know nothing. If you had not told me, I would forever have believed that one early morning I'd come across a demon in this field.' Soon we came to the crossroads; he showed me the way to Kragujevac, while he set off for Palanka.

I arrived in Kragujevac on the morning of 2 December. This town can be compared to a Slavonian village, with the difference that the main street in Kragujevac has a *čaršija* [bazaar]. Here I had my passport countersigned and, together with some men from Sarajevo, travelled by way of Čačak, Požega and Užice to arrive at the Serb *kontumac* [quarantine] at Mokra Gora on 5 December.

Talking of Čačak, I ought not pass over what I heard the Turks of Užice say about it. The church in Čačak was built by a *kaurin* king.[2] It subsequently became seven times a mosque and seven times a church. During a time when it was a mosque, there was a poor Turk who lived in a village. Though he was already fifty years old, he had never been to the mosque, except once as a child. One afternoon, however, he got the idea of going to the mosque. He saddled his horse, climbed into the saddle,

---

1. Their gloves are wide enough to accommodate the whole fist rather than having each finger separate.

2. *Kaurin* is derived from *djaur* or infidel. But the Illyrian Turks use the words in two ways. A *djaur* is a Serb or a Bosniak and every Turkish subject who is not of the pure faith, while *kaurin* is restricted to an infidel who is not an Ottoman subject.

and set off for Čačak for the noon prayers. He was the last to arrive at the mosque, after everyone else was already inside. He tied his horse and went to join them. But when he got to the door and looked inside he saw that every person was carrying a saddle on his back, and the *hodža* two. When he saw this he ran back, took the saddle off his nag, put it on his back, tightened it around his chest, and returned to the mosque to pray. When he got inside and the people saw him wearing a saddle they started to drive him out. He said: 'Why are you forcing me out when every one of you is carrying a saddle? Don't drive me away, don't beat me, don't you see the *hodža* with his two saddles?' This caused a big uproar; no one cared for prayers any more. Instead they tied his hands and took him to the *kadia*. They accused him of causing such a hullabaloo. The *kadia* asked him: 'How old are you?' 'Fifty,' he replied. 'How many times have you been to the mosque?' 'Only once,' he said, 'when I was a child.' 'Did you carry a saddle to the mosque then?' 'No,' said he. 'It was only when I saw that everyone was carrying a saddle and the *hodža* himself two. I therefore imagined that the practice had changed since then, and that everyone had to do so. This is why they have beaten me and brought me to you for judgment.' The *kadia* started to study the Qur'an in search of a possible explanation, found it indeed, and explained to the assembled people: 'That each person in the mosque carried one saddle and the *hodža* two means that each of you has one sin on his soul while the *hodža* has two. This poor man alone is innocent and may go home.' On hearing this each of them made him a gift, seeing that Allah had given him insight, and he was allowed to go home.

In the *kontumac* they examined our passports and let us

enter Turkey. When we came to Višegrad, Ajan Mujaga and the *kadia* of Višegrad had us arrested and locked up in what they called *Qur'antin* [quarantine]. One was supposed to sit in this *Qur'antin* for as many days as travellers to Serbia had to sit in the Serb *kontumac*. The Sarajevo merchants, however, already knew the *hadet*[1] and had brought *peškeš*[2] from Serbia for the Ajan and the *kadia*. Having received *peškeš* they let the merchants go, but I myself was kept imprisoned. I appealed to them, especially to Ajan Mujaga, who spent much time talking to me. He promised he would let me go to Sarajevo with the first merchants to pass by. The *kadia*, on the other hand, tried to persuade me to remain with him, saying that he would pay me well, more than I could make anywhere else, in return for which I would do no work other than translate for him, since he could read neither the Vlach nor the *kaurin* language. I told him that I liked my own trade best, which is why I wished to go to Sarajevo. I spent three days in the *Qur'antin*, but I was allowed to visit the *čaršija* and buy what I needed. There was a young man of my own age in the *Qur'antin* who had gone on business to Serbia, and now, on his return, had to spend ten days in confinement. There was no wood, so we told Aga Ibrahim that there was none. '*Valaha*, I'm not going to bring it to you,' he said. 'Go down to the *ahar* [stable], saddle the horses, and take yourselves to the hilltop.' We saddled the horses, took a small axe each, and set off for the hilltop, which was not far away. I was good at cutting the logs,

---

1. The Turks do not have established laws or rules, but refer only to *hadet*, i.e. custom. *Hadet*, however, is adjusted to suit them.

2. *Peškeš* is the gift of a bribe given to one's elders or someone of the same age. *Bakšiš* is the gift which an older person gives to a younger one as a reward for a small service. *Ajluk* is a gift earned, received from one's master as part of an agreement.

but how to load them was something only my partner knew. We repeated this three times. Fortunately merchants arrived who also brought *peškeš* for the *ajan* and the *kadia*, so on the second day of Bajram they let me go with them to Sarajevo across those forbidding mountains. But it would be good to say something here about Ramazan and Bajram too.

Ramazan is the fast preceding Bajram, which lasts as long as the number of moon-days, i.e. one moon cycle. During Ramazan Turks are not allowed to taste anything, or drink water, or smoke a chibouk; indeed they must guard even against swallowing their own saliva. In the towns a cannon sounds in the evening, after which they sit down to eat; they may eat throughout the night whatever they may have: meat, cakes or whatever. In the morning an hour before dawn the cannon fires again to wake up those Turks who wish to eat before sunrise. For as soon as dawn breaks the cannon sounds again, the *hodže* start reciting *sabah sabu* in the mosques, and everyone abandons food. Those who were late in eating must also stop as soon as they hear the gun. In the evening, when the *hodža* is to recite *akšam*, he lights the lanterns on the mosque, which he will have extinguished at some point in the night. In the morning, at about five o'clock European time,[1] he climbs up and lights the lanterns, which burn until the day breaks.

In the villages, where there are no cannon, they regulate themselves by dawn and sunset, and often go astray, especially in the morning when they oversleep. In the morning when starting their repast they rush out all the time in great worry, and look

---

1.   Turkish clocks (*sahati*) work differently. In the evening, a few minutes (*dekikah*) after sunset, the Turkish clock must show twelve, otherwise he moves it by hand to the right place; and so every day.

up to the sky to see if dawn is about to break, when they leave off the food. They suffer most from not being able to smoke a chibouk during the day: thus the *gazde* [household heads] spend much of the day asleep in order to ease the passage of the day and not think about a chibouk. When a Vlach friend comes to visit, they offer him as is customary coffee and a chibouk, as well as food, and then go to sit in a corner whence they converse with their friend. On the eve of Bajram the better-off farmers bear gifts, which they leave with the *kadia*, for the one who first sees the new moon in the sky. When the weather is cloudy, not all towns celebrate Bajram at the same time. Everyone watches the sky and, when they see the moon (there must be three of them together), they run off to the *kadia*, place their hands on the *ćitap*,[1] swear that they have seen the moon, and receive a *muštuluk* [reward]. The *kadia* then sends messengers in all directions announcing that tomorrow is Bajram. On the day of Bajram the guns sound and young men fire their rifles all day. The celebration lasts five days, though only three among gentlefolk. Those who cannot put off working may work all day without committing a sin, while at home a splendid dinner is prepared for them. Bajram comes twice a year, in the autumn and in the spring – the latter being called Korban or Kurban (Great Bajram). This is the only religious holiday the Turks have, setting aside Friday. On that day they work as usual, but are bound to attend the mosque and pray at least once a day. The Serbian Turks do not wait for Bajram until they see the moon in the sky, but ask a Vlach to find in his calendar the change of

---

1. The *ćitap* is a book on which they swear by laying their hands on it and saying: '*Valaha bilaha*, I saw this or that.' He did *ćitap*, i.e. he took an oath.

moon, and make that day Bajram.

When we arrived at the gates of Sarajevo, the Turks searched me and took me to Mustaf-pasha Babić, known as Hrnja (Hrnjaković). He questioned me about what I did and whence I came. I told him which part of Germany I was from, that I was an artisan, and that I wished to find a place in his celebrated country where I could settle down. 'For some time now I have wanted', said the pasha, 'to invite such masters here to Sarajevo and provide them with *halat* [tools], so that they may work. This is what I intend to do. In the meantime, however, until I manage to get the *halat*, and company for you too, you may remain here with me at the *kapia* (where all the lord's servants and courtiers gather).' 'What shall I do', I asked, 'here at the *kapia*, honourable pasha?' 'Do you smoke a chibouk?' Though I had not smoked it up to that time, I said that I did. 'Well then, since you smoke, you can sit where the others sit and smoke like the others smoke.' And so on that very day, 11 December, I began taking *tain*[1] and *jemek* (food) of nine or ten dishes, all prepared in the Turkish manner.

---

1. *Tain* is a bread roll made by an *ekmedžija* (baker) weighing about half an *oka*. All *nizami*, *spahie*, lord's servants and courtiers get two rolls apiece, i.e. one *oka* of bread per head. The Sarajevo *ekmedžije* take turns to deliver *tain* to the pasha's court, one each day, after which they can relax until their turn comes again. The same is true for *kasapi* (butchers) and their meat. None of this is paid for. When a new person arrives, the *sarajdar* turns up to demand whose turn it is that day. He tells the person that there is another one among them, so he has to deliver more. I do not know what *jemek* means in the Turkish language; I heard it only in lordly palaces and it means something like a meal. When I asked them what it meant they said food. When they eat or offer food they say *bujrum*. For example, if someone comes to you when you are eating he says *bujrum*; and you invite him to join you by saying: *Otuk bujrum*, meaning 'sit down and eat'.

Sarajevo is an enormous city: the people of Sarajevo themselves do not know how big it is, since no one visits every part of it. It is not permitted there to venture outside the main streets, not even to cast a glance anywhere, let alone enter. The *čaršia*[1] is huddled together beside the River Miljetska (Miljacka), with the exception of a few grocers (*bakali, bakalini*), artisans and bakers (*ekmedžie*) whose shops are found on the main streets. The inhabitants of each *mahala* can go freely following their own routes to the *čaršija*, but are strictly forbidden to enter another *mahala*.[2] Atop a hill at the first level of the mountains stands a modest albeit quite extensive fort (one might conjecture that it was originally erected for penning cattle in summertime, to prevent them from straying). It now contains Turkish houses with only one street (*sokak*) leading from the gate that is free for all to use. From its lower gates one can see the immeasurable expanse of Sarajevo. In between the houses, where we have squares they have graveyards: in sunlight the white stones of the *turbe* shine like so many swans.[3]

---

1. *Čaršia* means marketplace. According to the importance of the town, it may occupy one, two or three streets. But in Sarajevo itself all is in one huddle: on a spacious square there are wooden stalls in the manner of a European fair, the difference being that the alleys between the stalls are also covered with timber, so that people do not get wet. It is always dark inside these.

2. Turkish streets are not straight like European ones, but wind about and contain various sections. They are called *mahale* (villages). The ground alone on which one walks is a *sokak*: the collection of houses together with the *sokak* form a *mahala*.

3. A *turbe* is a grave that is fenced off and covered from above. The stone pillar with a *čalma* at the head of the grave is called a *bašluk*. When an *aga* dies, his family normally bury him in the courtyard or in the garden, but if they do not have space there they bury him beside a road, where people pass by. They cover the grave and its surrounding with neat slabs and

Below the fort a huge cliff overhangs the Miljetska. The Miljetska, which flows beneath the cliff, is formed from a multitude of brooks at the base of the Romania mountain and runs through underground caverns beneath Brezovača before reaching the centre of Sarajevo. Thence it flows through the outskirts until it disappears into the Bosna. The place below the above-mentioned cliff beside the waters of the Miljetska is called Ašik Mahala. The Turks say that young men and women used to gather there in the old days to play various games. The best dressed among them was the beautiful Fata, loved by a slender youth by the name of Mehmed. His only care was to win Fata's favour. Knowing his wish Fata too started to long for him. One day the girls came on their own with Fata among them and started to dance a ring dance under the cliff by the water. When the youths in the town, including Mehmed, heard that they were dancing by the water, they all rushed to the top of the cliff to

---

build a low wall around this. They erect four posts at half-ell intervals, then join these up to form a roof, which they round off, sometimes leaving the work seemingly incomplete. In the middle of the posts stands the *turbe* (*bašluk*). Carved on this – especially in the case of old graves – is a sword or a sabre; or else a *buzdohan* [club], or a *topuz* (a *topuz* is a hollowed iron ball attached to a cornel-wood club). For as long as the dead man's line continues, each Friday a lamp is lit above the *turbe*.

They say that Mehmed Sokolović, pasha of Bosnia, after making his brothers Turks by granting them *spahiluks* [estates] and building them houses, tried to persuade his father too to become a Turk. His mother had converted immediately, but the father never accepted the true faith, saying: 'I will die in the faith in which I was born.' Following their deaths, Mehmed erected monuments to them: for his father as an infidel he placed an arch over two columns, and for his mother, in line with Turkish custom, a vault on four columns with a *turbe* in the middle. The Mehmed-Sokolović *han* has fallen into ruin, leaving only a broken fountain. The Turks told me that it takes a quarter of an hour from the road, i.e. that between Višegrad and Sarajevo, to the Sokolović place.

look. The beautiful Fata looked up and saw her beloved sitting like a hawk on the cliff. She waved at him with a golden scarf as if inviting him to join the dance. Confronted suddenly with this sign of her favour, carried away by great joy, he slid down the cliff and fell into the middle of the ring, killing himself before he could say *medet*.[1] Seeing his ardent love, Fata dropped on top of him, wishing only to utter his sweet name; but her heart broke from sorrow. The news quickly spread through the town, and all manner of people hastened there to see this sad event. Not one who came failed to kiss the two gently and weep bitterly over them. Their family and friends dug a grave and buried them together in it, like two most beautiful doves. From that time on, girls have been forbidden to join any public dance.

These days no one goes to Ašik Mahala, except for vulgar, shameless rakes, with whom this is how it goes. In the evening the rakes gather at Ašik Mahala, and as each arrives he sits down beneath the cliff and smokes a chibouk. When the crowd grows large, one will call out: '*Valaha*, my good fellow, what are we to do now?' Then they start boasting about who among them knows some bad and cowardly Vlach with a beautiful wife. Then they divide up into groups, and each group goes off to visit its Vlach. They are not allowed, however, to bother a free Vlach while he is alive. If he has a particularly beautiful wife, the Turks first try to kill him, after which his widow is at their mercy. The girls to whom nature has bequeathed beauty are the most unfortunate, since no Christian youth is allowed to look at them, let alone marry them. As a result the most beautiful ones are forced to become Turks. I once heard some Turks talk about this, saying:

---

1. When dying the last word Turks say is '*medet*', just as Christians say 'Jesus.'

'There are many beautiful girls also among the Catholics, but they refuse to convert. It is the fault of the friar, the *dženabet*.[1] If a poor girl decides to convert, as soon as the friar learns of her intention he immediately calls her to mass and there berates her, seeking to dissuade her from it. If she does not obey, he drives her in shame out of the community, and when the others see this hardly any is willing to convert.'

I heard also of a distressing case that happened recently. A baker of the Eastern [Orthodox] faith had a most beautiful daughter, tall like a green pine. But she could not marry a Christian, while she resolutely refused to convert to Islam. Thinking day and night about her misfortune, she withered like a pine whose roots had been cut, and finally died. The Turks felt great sorrow for her, saying: the poor girl would have converted, but her family and parents did what they could to dissuade her.

Every honest youth goes *ašikovati* round the house of his *milostnica* [favourite].[2] Some court for two or three years, especially if the father is against it. When the young people realise that her parents are absolutely refusing to permit their marriage, they agree among themselves: one night she collects as many of her clothes as she can manage and runs to her darling. Her father grows very angry, and sometimes spends three or four years thinking how to exact bloody revenge against his predatory son-in-law. But the more angry he gets, the more his son-in-law

---

1. In Bosnia a *dženabet* means a good-for-nothing, scoundrel or trouble-maker.

2. *Ašikovati* means to court. Hence Ašik Mahala, i.e. the place or village of courting. *Milostnica*: since Turks may have many wives, the most beloved is called the favourite. So too Christians, if one has a true wife but keeps company with another, say: 'There goes his favourite [mistress]; he keeps a mistress and cares not for his wife.'

avoids him. As time goes by, either the father-in-law realises that he cannot win, or he calms down of his own volition and makes up with him, after which they hold a wedding feast.

Courting frequently leads to injury, particularly when two court the same girl. This, however, does not happen close to the girl's house, in order to prevent it coming out; but one confronts the other in the dark, even in another *mahala*, as he passes by, and applies his *kustura* (a supposedly blunt knife) to his throat. Courting, they say, is always dangerous, because there are also the *bekrijah* (tramps, rough types) who wander around at night seeking someone to knife. They say one may frequently find of a morning some youth lying in the *sokak* who has everything about him – weapons, money, nice clothes and a watch in his bosom – lacking nothing but his head. The one who killed him sought only to get blood on his *kustura*.

It was a bitter winter in Bosnia. A [Tartar] courier arrived from Travnik with an order that all the pashas of Bosnia had to gather at the vizier's residence. So on 18 December we too (around thirty of us) set off for Travnik with the pasha and his son Miralaj [colonel] Mula Ibrahim, every one of us riding a *menzul* horse, and leading three of the pasha's horses as *jedeki*.[1] The road was dreadful and we rode in the Tartar manner (fast). Since it was very cold, I took my legs out so that they would not become frostbitten from the *uzendije*.[2] At some point my horse's

---

1. *Jedek* means a number of different things: 1. a spare horse taken because of its beauty; 2. string, rope; 3. dishes used in inns; 4. church dishes are called church *jedeki*.

2. Turkish *uzendije* or stirrups are large and enclose the whole foot like a shovel. One corner sticks into the horse in the manner of a spur. *Mezul* is mail; *mezudžia* a postmaster; *surundžia* a postman. A *mezulhana* or post office has around fifty horses, its own or rented from peasants for the use

front legs bowed, and he bent his head and neck and threw me over, so that I flew an ell beyond his head. I took fright, thinking that the horse had broken his front legs and I should have to continue on foot, but the Turks began to laugh, saying I had jumped as if from the sky. My horse then got up and I mounted him, and so it continued from one *mezulhana* to another until we reached the *kadija*'s court at Visoko, where we were to stay the night.

As we travelled through the Sarajevo *pashaluk,* peasant Turks came before the pasha to complain that they suffered from injustice in the same manner as the *raja* [Christian folk]. In order to get rid of them the pasha told them to send their elders to Travnik to testify before the vizier and other pashas, and that they would certainly have their troubles eased. The Turks kept visiting Travnik after that, but got no response to their complaints.

Once in Visoko every Turk had to bring something for our supper and hay for our horses, as was the custom when *nizami* and *spahie*[1] passed by. Some brought roast lamb, some a turkey, some a pie, some bread, some cabbage and meat and various sweetmeats, but mainly rice and pasta. The food that we were given could have fed a whole company of Austrian soldiers. The rooms suddenly filled with Turks who began to eat. It is impossible to describe their eating habits, how they fought and pushed each other. The hungriest and wildest wolves could not

of travellers.

1. *Nizami* are regular infantry, *spahie* cavalry or hussars who own their horses and buy their own riding dress. Their saddles, to which two pistols are attached, come from Hungary. They carry a sabre attached to their waist and a spear in their hand or attached to their shoulder. When the *nizami* and the *spahie* pass, the municipality is obliged to feed them.

by far be compared to them, let alone compete with them. It was very Turkish! They rent the meat apart with their fingers, and those who got hold of a piece would not let go of it, but would swallow it in one gulp as if thrusting it into his chest. Watching their behaviour but lacking the necessary skill, I remained quite hungry. But since no one was allowed into the pasha's room, the *kafedžibaša* gave me what was left on his table, aware that despite the abundance of food my appetite had not diminished. The following day, on 19 December, we arrived in Travnik and put up at Filipović-beg's house. We stayed with him for ten days.

The pashas, accompanied by their retinues, met twice a day at the vizier's. There is a large *džamia* [mosque] in front of the vizier's house which has retained a square tower[1] with a Turkish clock on it. I might say that this was once a monastery, but anyone who said that this was once a church would be executed. Travnik is a small, elongated town lying in a hollow between two mountains, with the small River Lašva flowing through it, beside which stand several little mills and presses, including one mill whose wheel bore ladles as is common in Croatia, with the water flowing beneath. This watermill is highly appreciated here, as if it were a steam engine: only merchants and *age* are allowed to approach it, each saying in wonder: '*Valaha*, this is a *murafet* – a mill wheel that turns like a grindstone.'[2]

---

1. A *džamia* is small and mainly round or at least a perfect square. A *munara* is thin like a chimney, tall and round, sticking far above the *džamia*'s roof. It stands to the right of the door, the only exception being the Begova Džamija in Sarajevo, which because of its awkward location has its *munara* on the left side. The *džamija* in Travnik must once have been a church.

2. Turkish mills are very crude. A tree trunk serves as the axle (*Mühlstange*); at the end of the trunk is a wheel with wooden bowls into which the

The fort stands on the side under Mount Vlašić, and a spring rises beneath it too. I did not dare go to the fort, because the others were already suspecting me and planning to denounce me as a spy. A friar came at Christmas to Travnik to conduct the Holy Mass and preach the word of God, and I went to hear him. The poor friars do their best to keep the people away from Muhammad's faith (and evidently before their own people speak against Muhammad and his religion). When I returned home, Filipović-beg asked me in front of all the Turks: 'What did the *prator* (as they say) speak about during the mass?' 'Nothing,' I said. 'He conducted the mass.' 'Why,' he said, 'do you think that I don't know? A prator never said mass without abusing Turks and Muhammad.' 'A prator is but a prator,' said another, 'he may do as he likes.'

In the town of Travnik, the Christians are banned from conducting God's service, but they may do so outside it. For Christians of the Roman confession, the mass is conducted by a friar (when he comes) at a nearby hill in a better-off house. Christians of the Greek faith, since they have no house on the hill, must observe the mass under a tent; it is quite awkward for them to have to carry round the tent and the holy items. And when the rain and generally atrocious weather comes, they are all outside except for the priest. Often, as they prepare to conduct the mass, there is something they have forgotten to bring, so they have to shout from above, for example: 'Hey, Marko, bring the book and the lantern and this and that!' This is hard on the poor people.

There was once here a young Turkish widow whose husband,

---

water falls; and on top of the trunk sits a stone turning round at the same time as the wheel.

having no children, left everything to her, making her rich. Our Husein-čauš, who was also a *većilašćia*, somehow learnt about her and went to court her. During the whole time in Travnik we never got any of the sweetmeats to which we had been accustomed in Sarajevo. We also noticed that each evening the *većilašćia* would carry an array of covered dishes somewhere. The *kavazi* followed him once to see where he was going, and saw that he was taking them to the young widow. The informers returned to say that Husein-čauš was courting the widow. Voices broke out among the *kavazi*, some saying: 'So that's what he's doing, feeding her ... with our provisions.' Others said: 'Never mind, we'll report him to the pasha and he'll impale him.' Still others said: 'No, the pasha will not execute him the first time round, particularly since he'll say that he'll marry her. It's better that we ambush him and cut him down.' They all agreed, sharpened their knives, primed their guns, and arranged among themselves who would form the ambush. They then set off I know not whither, but they soon came back, whether because they feared that the pasha would subsequently execute them, or because they feared Husein himself. Husein was about forty years old, tall and bony as an oak trunk. His chest, arms and legs were covered in hair like a wolf and he had a weird look in his eyes, as though he were a seer. But he nevertheless appeared a peaceful man. And then the *kavazi*, like all Turks, at one moment live like brothers and only a moment later seek to break each other's necks; so Husein soon learnt that the *kavazi* had intended to ambush him. Husein also learned that in the evening, after the pasha had gone to bed, the *kavazi* would go to the inn to drink *rakia*, and resolved to have his revenge. One evening, after the pasha had gone to bed and the *kavazi* had as usual set off for the inn, he set up an ambush for them. They reached halfway, but the night was unfortunately very bright so one of them saw him and shouted: 'There's Husein!' – whereupon they all fled. Seeing that he would miss them, Husein chased them with a naked blade, but failed to catch up with them. The following day the *kavazi* talked the matter over in their room and cursed about how Husein had done them wrong and was trying to ambush and kill them. Husein heard this, went to the room of the *kavazi* and told the one believed to be the bravest man among them: 'Listen here, you in your *ćulaf*![1] Don't curse, since you know it was only by chance that you weren't left lying dead from my knife in the middle of the *čaršija*. You should also know that you won't die in your own way, but are to be downed by my right hand.' Having said this he left and closed the door behind him. The *kavazi* were shocked more by his terrible eyes than his thunderous voice. I myself was quite astonished at the freedom with which this was being said. Elsewhere in Europe, such words alone could cost a man if not his life then his liberty, whereas here no one cared. When the *kavazi* regained their composure, rather than harbouring a burning desire for revenge, they instead succumbed and started to defend him, saying to one another: 'He's right; who can forbid him to do what he wishes and to take the wife he wants.'

---

1. A *ćulaf* is a cap moulded from wool which the Turks, after taking off the *čalma*, put on their head in order to avoid catching cold. They sleep at night with the *ćulaf* and take it on their journeys. Since Turks began to set aside the *čalma* (i.e. when they became *nizami* [foot soldiers]) and to wear a great fez, some of them to keep warm wear a *ćulaf* underneath it, while others line it with cotton wool. A fez is a red cap; the *nizam*'s or great fez is large enough to contain one of our caps.

There was a mad ancient in Travnik (possibly from Dalmatia, because he could speak some Italian) whom the others called the mad *Švaba* [German]. He tottered about the streets behaving in a crazy manner. The pashas and some *age* would give him a *bešluk* (5 Turkish groschen) apiece to beat the town Vlachs with his cudgel and drill them in the German manner. Seeking to please them, he would keep close to our house and, when poor Vlachs came by, he would run after them shouting: 'Halbrechts, halblinks, hullo, march!' And the Vlachs would flee. Once a Turkish peasant came by with horses carrying wood for sale. The *Švaba*, thinking he was a Vlach, rushed after him hoping to scare him. When he saw that the Turk stood his ground, he used the thick part of his cudgel to beat him, shouting: 'Halbrechts, halblinks, hullo, march.' The Turk now wished to run away, but felt ashamed seeing that so many *age* were looking at him. So he raised his head and stared at the *Švaba*, shouting: 'Go away, sirrah cross, go away sirrah lime-wood cross!' But sirrah cross would not listen, hitting him instead ever harder with his cudgel. When the Turk saw that sirrah cross had begun to lash out in earnest, he ran to his horse, took hold of his load and tried to pull a log from it to defend himself; but sirrah cross continued to hit him from behind. Having had enough of the cudgel and being unable to free a log, the Turk left his horse and fled to the shop of a Turk. Once inside, he borrowed a big knife (*hanžar*) and ran out to cut up the *Švaba*; but our *Švaba*, on seeing the Turk wielding a knife, forgot that he was lame and infirm, and unfolding his legs like a deer he escaped across the bridge, leaping like a doe.

On 30 December at around seven o'clock Turkish time, it

being time for lunch, the *véćilašći* called upon us to come and take *tajin* and *jemek*. But a courier suddenly arrived from Sarajevo and told the pasha that a rebellion had broken out in Sarajevo, and that the rebels were planning to kill his wives and children and set fire to his court. The pasha ordered that we should promptly cease what we were doing, mount our horses and ride at top speed back to Sarajevo. The *surudžie* brought round the *mezul* horses and everyone immediately mounted them, leaving me with one that carried the worst saddle: I was also to lead a *jedek*. In a field below Travnik there is a stone bridge, which like all Turkish bridges is not banked up with earth at the sides, so that one is obliged to climb first up then down the arch. As I was moving across the bridge, my *jedek*, being fresh and playful, wished to prance there, but I restrained him by holding on to the harness. When he pulled harder, the girth on my horse snapped, and the saddle and I tumbled to the ground. The *jedek* took fright, and since I was holding him tight nearly trampled upon me. The pasha and his retinue sped on across the field; only the *kafedžibaša* and the *berberbaša* jumped from their horses in order to help me, while Omer-čauš remained with us astride his horse. He was my worst enemy, one who, fearing that the pasha might neglect him in favour of me, sought every opportunity to do me down. Having been reprimanded three times by the pasha, he felt the time had come to realise his evil intentions. The *kafedžia* and the *berberin* wanted to resaddle my horse, while I held the *jedek* and their two horses. We had no cord, however, with which to bind up the broken girth. Omer-čauš suddenly drew his sabre, saying: 'You wretch! It would have been better if your mother had given birth to a stone rather than to you!'

The *kafedžia* caught his horse; he quickly dismounted, wishing to proceed on foot, but the two held him. 'Let me cut up the wretch!' he said. 'Don't! Sober up!' they said. 'It would be *jazuk* in the eyes of God, since he has done no harm to anyone.' 'He's a *nesrečnik* [wretch]:[1] if he were not one, the girth would not have snapped under him. Let me go!'

I for my part was leaning against the horse, calmly watching if they would let him go. I recalled that each horse carried two pistols, with one of which I should be able to get him. But they did not release him and forced him to calm down. They managed somehow to tie the harness, I remounted and made haste across the field. When I looked back and saw that the others were hanging behind, I slowed down for them to catch up. When they closed in Omer-čauš once again made a thrust in my direction, drawing his sabre halfway, but then as if having considered pushed it back in again. The *berberbaša*, seeing that I was still imperilled, took off his sabre and gave it to me, saying: 'Here, carry my sabre for me, my lad!' He told the others: 'Faith, I have a boil here which does not let me even carry a sabre.' When Omer-čauš saw me carrying the sabre, he stopped threatening me. On our arrival at Busovača for the night, he said at supper: '*Valaha, bilaha*, by my Turkish faith, the *šejtan* entered my mind, that I should kill him.' 'Do not do it!' the others said. 'Dear Allah would never forgive you. It is a great sin to kill a youth, even though he be a Vlach, who has done no harm to anyone.'

I should add that it was bitterly cold during these days. I

---

1.   *Nesrečnik*: Bosnians, and especially natives of Sarajevo, use the term to denote a sly man, wicked and depraved, whom even dear Allah is unable to bear any longer. *Šejtan* is the devil; *jazuk* is sin; *halal/halaliti* is to forgive, to let go.

thought I would freeze to death on my horse. I felt quite hollow inside, and that the wind was blowing through my ribs and chest as if through a basket. I lost all feeling in my hands and feet: they no longer felt cold. I was bothered in particular by my shoulders and spine. It seemed to me as if all my bones and joints had come apart, leaving me to wonder what was holding my head, since everything else had gone. On arriving at our night quarters, we would dismount with great difficulty, because our legs felt like wood. The Turks would hand over the horses to a Vlach and hurry inside, while I would stay behind in the *ahar,* walking around and rubbing my hands until my limbs loosened, after which I would follow them. After my veins had warmed up, I would shiver as if I had a fever.

On the second day we arrived at the pasha's *teferič*[1] in Rakovica. The Turks, who up to then had behaved with much courage, now began to speak of frostbite. On the morning of 1 January 1840 we went to the pasha's farm, where we made camp. The pasha could not simply walk into Sarajevo, for fear that he might get killed, but sent a courier to summon the people who were on his side to the farm, so that we might enter the town together.

While waiting for the troops to arrive from Sarajevo we were to have some lunch. The pasha sent a *tutundžia* to get bread from the *većil*; but the *veščilašči* told him that there was no bread. On hearing this the pasha became enraged and sent Omer-čauš to tell *većil* Husein that if he had no bread he would promptly be put to death. Omer went and told Husein as ordered, to which Husein replied: 'Can't you see this *kandžia* [whip] of mine,

---

1. A *teferić* is an elegant summer house; also, when in summer one goes to the fields or woods taking food and drink with one, people say: 'Let's have a *teferić*.'

you *ugursuz* [rogue]?' Omer said: 'I don't care; I told you as the pasha ordered me; it is the same to me, only your head will be off today.' Husein took up his *kandžia* and went for him, shouting: 'Off with you, you Herzegovinian cur! Have you come here to order us about? Go back to Herzegovina, you *ugursuz*!'

Omer fled to the pasha's house. On hearing the clamour the pasha himself came out to see what was going on, upon which the two halted. The pasha started to talk to Husein and to threaten that he would have him beheaded on the spot for being so stupid as to leave Travnik without taking even bread with him. Husein, however, did not flinch but responded to the pasha in a firm voice: 'How could I bring bread for you from Travnik, when I did not have time even to count the pots; and my fault is that all the pots must be accounted for.' The pasha, angry as a lynx, responded: 'It is necessary,' he said, 'to open one's eyes wide as a *findžan* to see why you get paid one hundred and fifty groschen a month, when you can't do the job for which you are responsible. Not to speak of what you annually steal and cheat from me.' Husein replied: 'What, me cheat you? When all this time we were in Travnik, the money I stole from you left me with only six cotton caps; and if you feel so strongly about them I'll give you those too.' Omer plucked up courage to say: 'There, you admit yourself you've cheated for the six caps. But what about the cheating that you won't admit? And for just a single *para* you've stolen from the pasha you deserve to be beheaded here and now.' Husein once again shook the *kandžia* at him, shouting: 'Go away, you rogue! You're no Herzegovinian, but a black Albanian cur. Come on, if you're so brave, and kill me!' The grave threats from the pasha had made no impression on

Husein; one might say he was not even very angry. But his darting eyes had instilled fear in all those who beheld him. The pasha himself, whether from fear of Husein or of the growing rebellion in Sarajevo, fell silent and returned to the house. I think that, had circumstances been different, Husein would have been beheaded. But it is also most likely that he would not have been the first to die, but would have first sent someone to the other world as his messenger before succumbing himself. As it turned out, however, a shepherd's wife, on hearing there was no bread, had made a round loaf and put it to bake; and while they were all quarrelling the loaf was ready. She then offered the hot bread to the pasha. Then the men from Sarajevo came, some 200 mounted Turks, and we set off with them for the city.

Sarajevo at this time was suffering from a great famine: that is what had caused the rebellion. The Turks said that the pasha had imposed an unbearable terror upon the *vilaet* [country] and had raised the level of *djumruki*[1] on all the roads: they said he taxed everything. 'And why are we taxed, as if we were Vlachs and not Turks like him?! This is why dear God does not send us *berićet*,[2] given that we oppress our own kind.' When the pasha arrived at his court, he quickly distributed money to a number of Turks to calm them down. Others he caught and at once had them 'shod', in other words beaten on the soles of their feet. When he had ended the rebellion, he started by command of the vizier to prepare for a journey to Fojnica, in

---

1. *Djumruki* are tolls of a kind, the level of which varies in accordance with the pasha's will.

2. *Berićat* is progress, as well as the harvest as a whole. *Berićatus* also means thank you: e.g. when an innkeeper receives money or a tip from you, he says *berićatus*.

order to visit the Roman bishop of Bosnia.

I myself, however, fell ill from catching that cold, while some of the Turks lost fingers from frostbite. A certain *surudžia* Harap lost all his fingers up to the first joint; Mehmed-aga lost two fingers on one hand and one on the other. The Tartar courier lost a toe and part of another. In this way each of them became maimed, whether in his hands or his feet. My hands and feet remained whole, but I became sick in another way. The pasha told me that I too would go to Fojnica. On hearing this, I thought I should not be able to survive such a journey; not even if I were healthy would I set off willingly, let alone in my sick state. So I said to myself that I would go to see the pasha and ask him to release me, after which I would take a cure somewhere in Sarajevo, and once recovered would travel all over Bosnia. At this point it was my back that hurt most, so much so that I was unable to lift my arm from the shoulder: I would not wish to cross myself with that arm, even if a thousand devils were suddenly to swoop down upon me. So I appeared before the pasha and said to him: 'Honourable pasha, you can see I am ill. This Bosnian air is very bad for me, so I beg of you to grant me *izum* to leave the *vilaet*.' He said: '*Peke, peke*,' and went to a room where he signed my passport. He gave this to the *ćehaja* to sign too and to affix a *mur* [seal]. When he gave me the passport he said: 'Let me give you some money.' He gave me 8 florins; I thanked him and left.

The pasha then said to the others: 'I shall see what he'll do: whether he'll return home, or whether he only tricked me and plans to remain here in Sarajevo. If he remains here, I shall order that he be flogged and take him back into my service.' A *sarajdar* [palace servant] (born in Srijem) followed me and told me what the pasha had said. As a result, instead of taking to my bed there until I should regain my health, I had to leave Sarajevo and move back to Serbia. I was very sorry that I was unable to realise my original plan, but I thought that, God willing, I should return to Bosnia at a later date. As it turned out, however, a serious illness prevented me from doing so. Omer-čauš, happy to see me go, accompanied me to the walls of the fortress, whence I traversed the fort alone and by way of Brezovača managed somehow to reach lodging for the night at Mokro under Mount Romanija on 19 January 1840.

I found nothing to eat or drink there, so I set off the following morning on an empty stomach to climb Romanija at Novakove Stjene [Novak's cliffs]. By the time I somehow managed to get up there, my limbs had grown quite numb. I was covered in cold sweat, I lost consciousness and fell down upon the snow beside the path. A light winter morning breeze was blowing, which pleased me greatly at the time. When I came round a little, I unbuttoned my jacket to cool down my chest, when a man (of Eastern faith) arrived, who together with his wife had taken three horses laden with wheat to sell in Sarajevo market; they were now riding back home and leading a third horse. When they caught sight of me, and saw that I was what they call a *Švaba*, they asked me where I had been and whither I was going. I told them that I had been in the pasha's service, and wished greatly to return home, but could not manage it.

They looked at one another. The man said: 'Wife, what shall we do?' 'Well,' she said, 'let him ride the horse to the other side of Romanija, after which it will be easier for him.' The man jumped from the horse, raised me a little, brushed the snow from me, and said to his wife: 'Give me the bottle from the saddlebag, Milica, so that the man may fortify himself a little.' She took out the bottle and I was made to take three gulps of *rakia*. He then lifted me onto the horse and we proceeded over Romanija. Let me tell you at this point something about this mountain.

Mount Romanija is very big: it takes around five hours to cross it by the established route (the distances are increased there by the bad roads). On the far (western) side from Sarajevo, it displays mighty cliffs: not even the healthiest of men can climb it here without a good meal inside him. A stone pillar with a kind of roof stands by the road there: here, people say, the watchguards Novak, Radivoj and Gruica always used to sit, and they would rob any traveller who did not bring them a gift.[1] They used to kill Turks without any compunction. The two brothers, Novak and Radivoj, were born in a nearby village; Gruica was Novak's son. They were great heroes and lived in caves on Romanija. One cave they turned into a kind of house. From somewhere they brought in an iron gate that they affixed to another – this was their *hazna*. People say that the doorway of the *hazna* remains well preserved: the Turks have over time taken away the iron grille, but there remain several stone pillars on the way in. Sarajevo sent several armies against them, especially Djerzelez-aga, but they vanquished them every time, because Romanija is unaccessible from that side. If nevertheless some mighty force arrived, they

---

1.　In memory of this, anyone who crosses Romanija for the first time in company must carry a log on his shoulder with which to shore up the stone, saying: 'to keep it from falling over'. This is why there are plenty of logs beneath it. But they first trick each novice by saying: 'There are watchguards sitting there who need logs to keep their fire going.'

simply left Novakove Stjene and withdrew deeper into the mountain, after which the Turks, finding nothing to do, would return to Sarajevo. Novak and his band would then return to the road. When Novak and Radivoj grew quite old and surrendered their powers to Gruica, Gruica one day went on his own to Sarajevo in disguise so that the Turks would not recognise him, in order to buy powder and lead and listen to the Turks talking. On his arrival in Sarajevo he made for an inn where Djerzelez-aga was drinking coffee in company, saying: 'Look, Novak and Radivoje have grown old, and they're no longer able to chop off Turkish heads; let's go and take our revenge on them now, since we couldn't get them in their young days.' When the begs heard this, they promptly sprang up and started to gather a great army. Gruica quickly took as much powder and lead as he could, and went to Romanija; he told his father and uncle there that a mighty army was moving against them, which they could not escape on account of their old age, but they should leave now while they could. They started to mock him, saying that he was a coward, that they had often met with Turks and won each time, and that today too they felt no fear. The army now arrived. They fought bravely at first, but since the Turks were pushing from all sides, Novak and Radivoj – vanquished more by their old age than by the Turks – perished together. Gruica could easily have escaped with the rest of the band, but wishing to save the lives of his father and uncle he was captured alive.

Djerzelez-aga granted him his life, upon condition that he cut down and burn all the trees on Romanija, so that the hajduks would no longer be able to find refuge there. This is why even today, when some scrub does appear on Romanija, the Turks set it alight out of fear that hajduks might find a home there. It is not difficult to burn it down, because no other trees grow there but small pines, and pines drip resin on the ground in summer. There is no water on Romanija other than the occasional cistern (a hollow used to collect rainwater).

Such are the stories I have heard on this subject, and that this is why they are still called Novak's cliffs. Arriving with my benefactor at a *han* [hostelry] on the other side of Romanija, I asked him to leave me there, telling him that I would remain there until I either grew well again or died. He took me off the horse and led me into the *han*, where he recommended me to Daga-spahia, saying that I was a sick man in a foreign land and that he should be *mukaet* (attentive) to me. Daga took me to his *kafana*, and I lay there on a carpet. His *hodža* asked me what ailed me and whether I would eat something. I told him I could not: I was thirsty, probably because of the *rakia*, and drank an enormous amount of water, which made me vomit. I vomited what I had eaten twenty days earlier in Travnik,[1] which the harsh cold must have preserved. After having vomited I practically fainted from weakness, while the *odadžija* emptied the *karlica* outside.[2] Some Turkish merchants arrived for the night, and when they saw me so very weak they asked me if I could eat anything, saying that they would pay for it. They told

---

1. I could tell this because of the apples, which I had not eaten since Travnik. Whatever I threw up appeared as fresh as if it had been in a goatskin pouch.

2. A *karlica* is a kind of vessel. The *odadžia* is the servant at an inn responsible for the rooms. A *bardak* is a copper vessel: it has a lid and a spout and contains around two *oke* (c. 2.5 kilograms); one drinks from it, takes water in it for ritual or everyday washing; and also takes it along when going to the lavatory. A *sevap* is a pious endowment, a charity.

each other it was great charity to help a sick foreigner. I had been left completely devoid of bodily strength; I lay like a dead log and could barely signal to them that I could not eat a bite, but I could hear what they were saying. The *hodža* bent over me and said several times: 'Pray to God, *komšia*,[1] pray in accordance with your own faith.'

I could not tell him that I could not, but he realised it nevertheless, so he took the Qur'an and started to recite from it. By the time he had finished reading the Qur'an, the *odadžia* had brought supper to the table. They sat down to eat, feeling sorry for me, a poor man ill in a foreign land, who would not live to see the next day. When they had finished their supper they started to recount various tales, at which time I fell into a slumber. I woke up when the first cocks crowed. I felt a little better and realised that I was hungry; but it was the worst moment of the night and I, being in a foreign house, could not bother the people too much. When in the morning the Turks got up to drink coffee, I asked the *kafedžia* to make one for me too, whereupon one of the merchants said: '*Kafedžia*, make him two with sugar; I'll pay!'

The worst thing in Turkey, especially in the countryside, is that even if they wish to be hospitable to someone, they have nothing to offer him except *proha* (maize bread), coffee and *rakia*. There are people there who have never seen wine, and who talk about this thing that can be found abroad that is called wine and those who drink it acquire a red nose like a turkey's. At this

---

1. When a Turk wishes to be polite he calls everyone, be they Vlach or German, *komšia* or else, especially in the Drina valley, 'Brother Serb'. They, on the other hand, must always call him 'Turk': e.g. 'God be with you, Turk!'

time I could not even get pickled cabbage, because the barrels had iced up. I managed to persuade Daga to use his axe to break off some ice and cabbage. He also cooked me some prunes. I spent three days at his place, when I felt a little better. I left on 23 January for Hanić, there to spend the night. Since the Turks do not have a mosque there, they had to pray in the room; but, since I was already there, they did not drive me out. As a result I saw there for the first time how the *hodža* goes to a corner facing east and the others gather behind. He first took the Qur'an and recited something from it, then set it aside and knelt and began to worship, with the others emulating his every move. But the *hodža* alone recites [*čati*[1]], while the others merely: say: '*Amin! Amin!*' But I wish to speak more about prayers later on.

From Hanić I went to Novakasaba [Nova Kasaba or New Town]. I took a great liking to this little place – were it not for the fact, dear brother, that it was purely Turkish. The whole area has the appearance of a garden, and in the midst of the garden Kasaba beside the River Jadar. There was a stone bridge across the river, which people here say was built by the *Kauri*. One of its sides has come down, but the other remains – sufficient to make it passable for horses or men following each other in line – but I fear this too will not last much longer under the Turks.

---

1. *Čatiti* is what the Bosniaks call reciting by heart, preaching. And while we talk about reading a book, they study a book. They say 'book' even when speaking of nothing but a piece of paper. The *hodža* on the minaret calls out without reference to a book; but they never say that the *hodža* recites the *saba* (morning prayer) but that the *hodža* studies the *saba*, the *hodža* studies the *podana*, the *hodža* studies the *ićindiu*, studies the *akšam*, studies the *jacia*, etc. And when the time comes for him to make his call, he comes in front of his house (if there is no mosque), climbs up a fence and starts to cry: *ićberila alah ilalah*, etc. *Alah ilalah* means dear God.

Here in Novakasaba I came across idle *kiridžie*, with whom I went riding on the following day. My greatest fear was that my horse might stumble on the bridge. We went from there across some ditches, then across fields until we came to a steep path called Zalac [devil]. When we started to climb up Zalac, the saddle slid back over the horse's tail and I found myself on the ground, while the horse carried on without the saddle. The Turks saddled him again, but I decided to climb up the hill on foot. This road fully deserves to be called Zalac, since it had made me believe it would take us right up to the heavens that day; but in fact we arrived only as far as the fort of Kuzlar, where we had to begin a climb down to a bigger pit than the one we had left. Kuzlar sits on a monstrous cliff above the confluence of the Jadar and the Drinjača. The Drinjača flows very strongly at this crossing, especially when the water is high, when travellers must wait for it to subside. When we were crossing it reached to the horse's belly, so that no horse could cross straight over but would be carried by the water a dozen feet downstream. Below this crossing the Drinjača flows into the Drina. On that day, 25 January, we put up at Kosirevo for the night. I paid the *kiridžie* their *kiria*, and left on my own for Zvornik.

Zvornik is a strange fortress: it starts below at the Drina, while up at the top a wall stretches from one crag to another. The fort is at its widest down at the Drina, but compelled by the crags it grows narrower as it rises higher. It is topped by a tower seemingly reaching into the clouds. The foundations of the fort's lower wall are bathed in water. The Turks say that when they were taking Zvornik from the *Kauri* there was a farsighted Kaurin *topčia* whose gun was called Zelenko. When the *Kauri* had to flee the fort before the advancing Turks, he placed a curse on his Zelenko and, after the Turks had entered the city, Zelenko suddenly leapt into the Drina. They wanted to pull it out, but it would not be dragged out, waiting for the infidels to return. Every time a war starts between the *Kauri* and the Turks, Zelenko thunders beneath the water. They also say that one day the *Kauri* indeed came and took Zvornik without much trouble, after which they proceeded to Višegrad with the intention of launching thence an attack on Sarajevo. When they came to Krvavac, however, a satanic army on horseback appeared before them: a flame issued from each horse's mouth, while each horseman's lower jaw hung down to the ground, while the upper coiled back over his head. Each of the soldiers grabbed an infidel by his leg, twirled him around and in an instant slew a hundred infidels. A great quantity of blood was shed there, which flowed into the Drina: from that time on the place was called Krvavac [*krv*: blood]. No one dares to walk that way by night, while even during the day, if one is alone, one may see some apparition.[1]

I took my passport to the pasha of Zvornik for his signature. The Turks do not know how to open a seal (because they only

1. Seeing an apparition [*prividěti*] is what the Bosnians say when a monster appears. When we were travelling to Travnik, we became a little late because of the bad roads and arrived in Travnik at ten o'clock in the evening European time. There is an old graveyard outside Travnik (the whole of Bosnia is covered with gravestones), where the pasha's son Miralaj had a vision. To begin with he saw something like a great and menacing eagle sitting on one of the *turbe*. He then looked up and saw above us a man flying backwards in front of him: each time Miralaj looked at him he bared his teeth. When we got to our lodgings in Travnik, Miralaj was as white as a seabass; it took a while before we could persuade him to tell us what he had seen. The Turks believed it all and, as further proof, quoted many similar stories from the old days.

stamp a *mur*): on seeing that my passport contained several seals, the *ćehaja* started to dig at one of the seals with his finger to see what it was made of. Worried that he might spoil it, I quickly tore the passport from his hands, saying that if he damaged it I should not be allowed to enter the *vilaet*.[1] The Turks were surprised by my action and began to whisper: 'How can a German be so free as to wrench a book from the *ćehaja*'s hands?' Another said: 'That's how the Germans behave at home too: they fear nothing from their masters.' One asked me aloud: 'Is it true that without that seal you would not be able to return home?' An old *aga* replied to him: '*Valaha*, he would have to run the gauntlet through two or three thousand men.'[2] The *ćehaja* then told me I could go.

I left Zvornik in the afternoon at around eight o'clock Turkish time, but when I got to the outskirts two *kavazi* came up to me and asked me for the *teskera* (passport). I showed it to them, but – unable to read the *teskera* and seeing that I was German – they became worried that I might be a spy, so they searched me all over to see what I was carrying. They found two maps on me and said: 'What is this then? Are you not a spy?' This gave me something of a fright. Waiting for me to say something, they grabbed one each with their fingers and pretended that they were about to tear them up: 'Talk, for otherwise we shall start

---

1. The Bosniaks do not say 'I go to my *vilaet*', but only: 'to *vilaet*'. Thus, for example, 'my *amidža* [uncle] has gone to *vilaet*; this is what *babo* [father] left me when he went to *vilaet*', i.e. to his homeland.

2. For the Turks, the gauntlet of birches is the greatest German cruelty. They say that the cursed German for the smallest transgression condemns a man to run a gauntlet of two or three thousand birches; and that the captain rides his horse the while wielding a sabre, and whomsoever fails to hit the poor man the worthless captain promptly cuts down.

tearing now.' 'Please don't, Turks, please don't, they're my icons, I pray before them.' 'Ahaa! *Peke, peke!*' they said, wrapped them up neatly and handed them back to me. They then told me to make haste, because the inn was far away and the land full of *hajduks*, and there was also a forest ahead of me. I gathered my things and hurried across the field, but did not manage to reach the forest before night caught up with me. I crossed the forest in darkness and arrived at a *mehana* to spend the night. They were surprised: whence was I coming so late? 'From Zvornik,' I said. 'But how come you managed to cross the forest without any trouble at all, when no one has done so before during day or night?' they asked. 'You were indeed very lucky.'

I set off from there in the morning and passed over the Janja, aiming for the Serb *kontumac* at Rača. After crossing the Janja it was *ićindia*,[1] and I thought I would spend the night at the village of Popovo [now Popovo Polje]. Walking across open country I met six Turks, and asked them – unfortunately! – the way to Popovo. And since a crossroads happened to be there – such was my luck! – they directed me away from the good road and into the forest. When I arrived in the forest and the night darkened, the road vanished little by little. I knew now that they had tricked me, but, dear brother, it was too late. I decided to continue walking through the forest in the hope of finding a house, as I had done in Croatia. But the forest was dense, full of logs and crevices, and I could not tell whether I was walking straight or in a circle. I three times encountered some animals

---

1.   Apart from noon, the Bosniaks give Turkish names to all parts of the day, as follows: *saba*, dawn; *ićindia*, evening service; *akšam*, darkness; *jacia* – which is two hours after *akšam* – Hail Mary. *Peke* means 'good, fine'. The Bosniaks call a spy *uhoda* and the Serbs *uvoda*.

which, when they realised I was a man, promptly scattered in all directions. At one point I came across a meadow, in which there was a haystack: I lay down in the hay planning to spend the night there; but the hay was as long as bulrushes and the wind was blowing from the north, so I realised that it was no good trying to sleep out in winter. I got up and moved on. I arrived at a low hill and heard dogs barking far away: there, I thought, I should soon reach a village if I followed in the direction of the dogs.

When I got near the village I found that the gardens were fenced off, and could not find any gap through to the village. By that time I had had enough of wandering around. So I jumped over a fence, thinking that this would be the quickest route. When I reached the garden I saw that there was no house there, so I jumped into another and again another. No sooner did I reach a courtyard than I heard a child cry out inside the house: 'Živan, Živan!' I knocked at the door, saying: 'God be with you, master of the house!' The child started to shout out even louder: 'Woe is me, Živan, help me, do!' Seeing that the child was scared of me, I decided to go to another house, but was unable to find the way out. At this moment the child's father rushed in from his brother's house, shouting: 'What's wrong, Milica? Why are you shouting?' 'Here,' she said, 'a man scared me.' 'But where's the man?' 'Here, in the courtyard.' 'Where are you, who scares my children?' he yelled at me without seeing me, for the night was dark. 'I didn't come to scare your children, brother,' I said. 'I'm a traveller who lost his way, so came to ask you if you'd let me stay for the night.' 'I know who you are, by God! I'll show you.' He ran into the house and came out again.

I wanted to run away but could not leave the courtyard, so I repeated my words, begging him in the name of God to let me stay the night. 'Nothing doing! No! I know who you are and why you're scaring my children.' With these words he lurched towards me and aimed something in my direction, saying all the while: 'I'll teach you to scare my children!' When I saw that he would not listen to me, I fell silent, calmly awaiting the deadly final blow, since I saw no way of saving myself. I even began to feel angry with him for scaring me, but not being ready to strike. I thought he was holding a knife in his hand, but it was a pistol, of which in that great hullabaloo he had failed to pull the trigger, so could not fire it. Wondering himself what was wrong with it, he thought it was broken and started to fiddle with the trigger.

His brother's wife now turned up to see what all the noise was about. He pulled at the trigger and started towards me, but the sister-in-law caught both his arms and started to shout: 'Don't, oh brother-in-law! Don't, oh brother-in-law.' He said: 'Go away, you bitch! I'll kill both you and him now!' The sister-in-law was strong, however: she gripped him hard and started crying for help: 'Woe is me! The man will die.' Her husband was the first to arrive, and after him the nearest neighbours; they managed to calm him down, arguing that I was a stranger who had lost his way and come to ask for lodging for the night. They all offered me a bed in their homes, but the man, wishing to expunge his shame, would not let them, saying that he was always glad to welcome strangers to his home. He said that he was drunk, that he had been drinking first with his relatives and then at his brother's house, and asked me to forgive him because it was the drink that had made him behave in that manner. 'But God would not let it happen,' he said, 'so you must come with me, because my house has what's needed to offer to a guest.' So he took me inside his house, and the people went on their way.

He told his children Živan and Milica what to bring me for supper, after which he started telling me: 'Look, little brother! This is my house and the one next to it is my brother's. I have two children – Milica and Živan, may the Lord keep them alive! – but my wife died no more than a month ago. There's a man here in the neighbourhood with whom I quarrelled long ago. He has a mother, an old witch, who threatens to eat all my family. I was visiting my late wife's relatives today. I almost burst into tears, and in order to comfort me they forced a good deal of *rakia* upon me. On my way home I called here on my brother, and he too produced a bottle of *rakia*. The two of us sat down and talked. My Živan came to tell me I should go home, because Milica was on her own. On the one hand she was pining for her mother, and on the other she remembered that accursed *baba* [old woman][1] and began calling Živan to come home quickly.

---

1.   The people here still believe (as is recounted for fun in our parts) that *babe*, who are witches, can assume any shape. When wishing to appear before people, they turn into some nasty beast. If they fear they may die in that shape, they turn into a human being, or if not quite confident in that form they change into wood or stone. They normally ride through the air in their female guise, after rubbing into their armpits a hellish paste that usually stands in a small pot carefully hidden under the hearth. In an unknown fashion they wrench the heart from anyone who crosses them and eat it. Having no heart, the victims must die within a day or two. If they wish to cause a person more pain, they devour in this way all his family and friends, leaving him alive albeit a cripple. This is why the man thought that the *baba* had taken his wife's heart; for which I, rather than the witch, almost paid with my head.

But when a witch finds herself in difficulty, such as had befallen me, she immediately changes into wood or stone, whichever appears best, depending upon whether there is more wood than stone at the spot, so that her opponent does not notice. If the opponent discovers under

At this very moment you knocked on the door, but the rest you witnessed for yourself, which you will not forget were you to live a hundred years.' Milica then brought the supper and Živan a bottle of *rakia*. Milica, a girl of twelve, being ashamed and convinced that the disturbance had happened because of her, refused to eat and used the time to make my bed. After having our dinner, we went to bed. In the morning my host brought out the *rakia* again, and took his leave of me. Then he showed me the way, and I arrived at Rača and the Serb *kontumac* on 27 January 1840.

I spent seven days in the *kontumac*, after which they gave me a certificate and I arrived in Šabac on 3 February. As for Šabac, I can say nothing more than that it is more beautiful than any other Serbian town except for Belgrade. There they signed my passport, and travelling via Palež I came to Belgrade on 6 February. Here my money ran out. I went to a master artisan to look for a job as a journeyman, and he took me on. I worked for him until 18 September 1840. On that day I got a headache, and on the following day a temperature that lasted for three weeks. After the temperature had abated, I fell into a high fever, and when that ended fifteen days later I needed only to set a scythe on my shoulder in order fully to resemble death. After recovering somewhat, I sought advice from my acquaintances on how to cross over to Germany and return home. They told me that since I had done nothing wrong, and since I was not from the

---

which guise the witch is hiding, he can easily kill her, provided he knows where her head is. Otherwise he can beat her for days without injuring her, until he strikes her on the head. If he strikes her on the head, she remains forever dead in the form which she had assumed.

My householder saw that I was not changing form, but nevertheless was suspicious because his pistol would not fire.

border, I should be able to enter the *kontumac* without further ado. So I went to have my passport endorsed at the consulate and the magistrate's court on 1 December, and left Belgrade on the 13th of the same month 1840.

When I arrived at the military headquarters they found me guilty of entering Serbia without permission, and handed me over to the town hall. There they assigned an orderly to take me to the civilian authorities for punishment. The penalty was actually of benefit to me, since in Srijem at that time wolves had eaten a man: without the orderly I would not have known the way, because it was snowing. I travelled from there by way of Vukovar, Osijek and Bjelovar and arrived happily in Zagreb on 7 January 1841.

Part II

Diverse Observations on Bosnia

*I*n the larger towns, all the better houses are walled round separately like forts, with *mazgale* (embrasures) built into the walls surrounding the courtyards. The gates to the courtyards are usually small, but in rare cases when the courtyard has a large gate it is always bolted.[1] Beside the gate (*kapia*) there is a *kapidžik* (little gate), and in one place I also saw stone teeth projecting outside the wall, which are used for climbing over the wall into and out of the courtyard. Inside there is usually a house in which the *saibia* (master of the house) resides, with the harem (the women's house) next to it. Alongside these are the *muftak* (kitchen) and the *ahar* (stable). Roses and other flowers grow in the courtyard, and if the master so wishes there is a *česma* (fountain). The rooms have no furniture, but a floor covered with *ćilimi* (rugs); under the *ćilimi* are *muntavi* or *muntapi* (floor coverings made of cord), and under the *muntavi*

---

1. In the doorway, half an ell above the ground, there is a hole in the doorpost that goes deep into the wall. This hole contains a beam: when the door is closed, the beam is pulled out and drawn across the door to the other doorpost. A peg is inserted between the beam and the frame, to make it stronger. This beam is called a *mandala*.

rush matting. Along the *duvar* [wall] beneath the rugs there are *dušeci* [woollen mattresses], and against the wall are propped pillows. They sit here during the day and sleep at night. During the day, the nightclothes are kept out of the way in a *dolaf* or *dolap* (wardrobe).

The rooms have ceilings low enough for a tall man to strike with his head. The ceilings in the rooms are made of timber finely carved by *degramadžie* (carpenters). A shelf (*rafa*) runs along the walls around the room. Inside the door the *dolap* runs across the whole breadth of the room, and appears also to contain the stove. At the doorway itself, the *dolap* forms an arched passage. Within the *dolap*, beside the stove is an *amandžik* (basin), and on the other side of the stove the formal dress is kept. The windows are set low, and rarely have glass, but are usually stuck over with paper. The windows of the harem have wooden bars on the outside.

In simple rooms the stoves are lit from inside, because of the coffee that is continually made and for the chibouk. A cauldron is built into the stove, to heat water for the *abdes* [ritual ablution]. Wealthy houses contain a room where coffee is made for the household and for those who come to visit, which is called the *kafana* or *kafeodžak*. There is also a room for saddlery and various weapons, which is called the *saračana*. A storeroom at ground level holds all kinds of useful things and is called a *magaza*. Next to the *divanhana* [hallway], there is a place where they normally wash and perform *abdes*.

Poor houses have fences all around. In the middle of the courtyard is a small house with, say, two rooms: one for the men and one for the women. In the courtyard they usually grow maize, pumpkins, watermelons and melons. Even in towns the houses do not form terraces, but each stands alone in the middle of the courtyard, so that one can walk all around it. If one should occasionally find a house that, due to the smallness of its courtyard, abuts onto the street at one end, it would have no windows overlooking the street, but only the usual embrasures. The courtyards alone of the individual houses can touch one another. The streets are always crooked and usually narrow.

In towns the places where travellers stay are called *mehane*. They normally have just one floor: an *ahar* at ground level, and bedrooms on the upper floor. A village or roadside inn where travellers may rest is called not a *mehana* but simply a *han*. A *han* is usually pretty dismal, so that anyone who has to spend a single night there in wintertime will never forget the word *han*. Every day the *handžia* prepares some wood for the travellers, which by the evening is all used up, so that the travellers are forced by the extreme cold to sleep like cats in the ashes in order to keep warm. In the morning the *handžia* turns up and says: 'Come on, people, time to pay for the heating!' The heating, paid per person, costs 1 groschen, i.e. 40 *pare*. It often happens when one arrives for the night that the wood is wet or green, and refuses to be kindled. People sit round the fireplace, wherever they manage to grab a place. When the wood does finally catch fire and begin to burn, the one who has got himself the best seat finds himself in great trouble, since the heat drives him away but the others stop him from moving back. If he gets up and moves to one side, he will not see the fire for the rest of the night and will practically die of cold. If he remains in his place, however, he is bound to be burned alive. Either way, if he survives he must pay for the heating next morning.

The part of Bosnia I have seen has many mountains, but between them lie beautiful lands, most of which are – alas! – left fallow. Generally speaking Bosnia is a fertile land, as is testified to in particular by the abundance of fruit. When I was in Sarajevo, there was famine there: an *oka* of wheat cost 60 *pare* and an *oka* of maize 50 *pare*.[1] Yet during the winter, an *oka* of apples cost 15 *pare* and one of prunes 30. But there are all kinds of other fruit too. The *rakia* sold in the *mehana* is rather expensive, and one is not allowed to bring in wine. If a *mehandžia* does obtain wine, he lives in great fear, since if discovered he will be severely punished. This is why he will sell a litre of wine for 2 groschen, i.e. 80 *pare*.

I have heard that Christians living in the countryside round Sarajevo fare worse than anywhere else in Bosnia. Christians there have nothing under the sun: neither house nor shelter nor cat. Everything in sight belongs to the *aga*. What they have are not houses anyway: houses are only for Turks, while the Vlachs live in baskets.[2] In autumn and spring the Sarajevan [*aga*] will give them seed for ploughing the land and planting wheat. At harvest time the Christian will mow, reap and thresh alone; and in autumn he will pick fruit, but always supervised by the *aga*'s man. He will share all this with the *aga* in proportions according to established custom.

Outside the Sarajevo plain, where Christians build their own houses, the Turks make sure that one of them does not build

---

1. An *oka* = 2¼ lb; our silver kreutzer = 7 *pare*.
2. A 'basket' is what the Turks call a Christian house made of wicker, woven like a basket and stuck together with mud. The roof is made of hay or straw.

himself a somewhat better house: if he does so, they immediately take him to court and ask: 'Why, sirrah cross, do you wish to have a house as if you were an *aga*? Off to the *aps* (prison cell) with you, until you pay so many hundreds of groschen. His house is to be taken from him and given to a Turk. A basket's good enough for you, sirrah lime-wood cross; go and make yourself a basket!'

In the Sarajevo pashaluk one is not allowed to keep pigs, and in Sarajevo itself not even to feed them in a sty. Taxes in Bosnia are paid by all who are not of the Muhammadan faith, whether they are inhabitants or not. When the time of taxes comes, even the freest of Frenchmen on a visit has to pay taxes, the same as a priest. The level of taxes is decided by the pasha.

In Bosnia the Illyrian language is spoken intermixed with Turkish words: there they '*eglendiše Bošnjački* [talk Bosniak]'. When they meet in the morning, they say: '*Saba hajrosum!*' and the response is '*Alah razosum!*' In the evening, to '*Akšam hajrosum!*' the response is once again '*Alah razosum!*' I have collected all the Turkish words found in this text and written them down in order [see Glossary]; I have also included those that are often first to appear in a conversation. If one wished to write down all the Turkish words that the Bosniaks use, it would make a whole fat book. They could express all their thoughts also in the pure Illyrian language, but one is simply unable to persuade them that [these words] are not ours but Ottoman. They at once say: 'No, you don't know Bosniak yet – they are Bosniak, not Ottoman. *Helbetum* (for example), when I say "*Saba hajrosum*", it means good morning, and you will reply "*Alah razosum*", which means God grant.'

Salam alećum may be said only by one Turk to another; and he replies *Alećum salam*. *Salam* means two things: greeting, and God bless you. God forbid that you [a Christian] call out *Salam* to a Muhammadan. I once made this mistake; had I not been a *Švaba*, I should have been in real trouble. But the others defended me, arguing that being a *Švaba* I did not know what I was saying.

The story goes that twelve Bosniaks of the Turkish faith were travelling together. They came to a field and saw some Ottomans riding towards them. Gripped by fear, they sought to discover if any of them spoke Ottoman, and one who was boastful said: '*Valaha*, I know Ottoman well.' So they let him go first. When they met up with the Ottomans, he quickly said: '*Salam alećum!*' One of the Ottomans replied: '*Salam!*' and asked him in Turkish how far the village was. But our Bosniak could say nothing further. This made the Ottomans angry, and they drew knives from their belts and began to curse: '*Anasine sitim, djaur pezevenk!*' The Bosniaks fled down a sidetrack with the Ottomans in pursuit. Thank God that there was a forest nearby, which enabled our Turks to live another day. However, once the Ottomans had turned back they began talking to one another about how Ottomans were evil people. The one who thought himself wise replied: 'Ah, didn't I tell you there were plenty more farts of every kind around *Salam*.'

In Bosnia the Christians are not allowed to call themselves Bosniak. When one says 'Bosniaks', the Muhammadans take this as referring only to themselves. The Christians are simply the Bosniak *raja*, or else Vlachs. Bosniaks and Ottomans, although both Muhammadans, in fact hate each other as if they were no brethren. The Bosniak hates the Ottoman because, he says, there is no worse man under the sun than the Ottoman; while the Ottoman says that Bosniaks, being *poturice* [converts], are worse than *djauri* [infidels], which is why they should be throttled and crushed. Woe to *poturice*! They should know who is in command. As a result the Bosniaks fear the Ottomans in the same way as Christians fear Bosniak Turks [Muslims].

I once asked some merchants who travelled all over European Turkey which was the language they used most. They replied: 'Wherever you go, you can speak Bosniak.' 'What about Istanbul?' I asked. 'In Istanbul,' they replied, 'it is mostly Bosniak, and only a little Ottoman and Greek.' But they are quite ignorant of the fact that they are mixing foreign words into their language, and insist that it is the Ottomans who mix in Bosniak words. The Bosniaks, in fact, use as many Turkish words as the [Slovene] people of Carniola and Styria use German ones, or even more I fear. They say that the entire Swabian [German] territory *eglendiše Bošnjački*, except for its most distant parts where real Swabians live; but that the language, my brother, has become corrupted by the Swabian tongue, which explains why they find it difficult to understand when they meet up with Swabians.

One may hear the true Turkish language less in Bosnia than in Serbia, because in Serbia the bazaar merchants regard it as a language of the educated, which is why every townsman speaks Turkish. In Sarajevo, on the other hand, there is many an *aga* who speaks nothing but Bosniak. Although the pasha of Sarajevo speaks Turkish, Arabic and Albanian very well, he does not like it when people converse in Turkish in his presence. If anyone says something to him in Turkish, he always replies in Bosniak, saying that 'our glorious Bosniak language is the most beautiful in the world'.

In Bosnia the most numerous are Christians of the Eastern confession, after which come the Muhammadans, followed by Christians of the Western confession. Jews are fewest of all, but they too are numerous. It is not necessary for me to speak about the Christian faith, because we have always been taught what the Christian faith is. But about the Turkish faith I can say the following:

Turks believe in God and in three prophets or saints: Moses, Iso Pejgamber (i.e. Jesus the Prophet) and Muhammad. Muhammad, however, is the best and holiest of all. A simple Turk knows nothing but that Muhammad is a saint, and that *šejtan* [the devil] will take those who do not firmly believe in this to *dženem*, to eternal fire. He who professes the true faith, however, will be taken by the saint to *dženet*, where dear Allah himself resides.

They practise circumcision like Jews, except that they cut off more flesh than the Jews. So according to law whosoever is circumcised must lie in bed for a month, until his wound has healed. During that month he may die of the injury, because they use no medicine, but merely sprinkle the wound with ash to stop the bleeding. During that month they have to fast day and night, i.e. during that time they must eat nothing but dry bread and fresh milk: even to drink water would desecrate the holy nature of the act. Some circumcise children while still infants, before they are fully conscious; but such young children become ill and die easily. Others leave their children until they are thirteen, so that they may be strong enough to survive the wound; but when they grow bigger they hate having to be circumcised like little children. Still others insist that it is better to circumcise a child when he is ten, because he is then neither too old nor too young for it.

The *hodža* never carries out circumcision, for there is a man skilled at this (called a *sunetži*), a groom, for example, who travels through villages and towns and carries out circumcisions. He throws a mattress on the ground, and the young Turk lies on his back upon it. This godly man has special pincers for the purpose, with which he grasps the skin at the end of the human flesh, pulls it like a true Turk and cuts it off with an *ustra* (razor), while others quickly sprinkle it with ash. The *sunadži* has to be paid 20 kreutzers, or three and a half groschen.

When a *djaur* wishes to become a Turk, he is first taken to a mosque where the *hodža* recites the Qur'an over him. After he has done, the convert must repeat something after him. The name they give him is his own choice. The other Turks present him with gifts, and when he comes home they circumcise him. Women find it easier to convert, because no wound is inflicted on them: they are converted at a mosque in accordance with the canon.

The *hodža* recites from the Qur'an that it is a great j*azuk* (sin) to rape a girl, greater than killing seventy-seven men. Whosoever has sinned this much must come to the mosque on Friday at seven o'clock to pray, with the *hodža* reading the Qur'an over him; the good Allah will then forgive. It is necessary to pay the *hodža* a sum agreed in advance.

Nothing is paid for the souls of the dead. One instead pays

the *hodža* or some other respectable man to recite from the Qur'an on a Friday at seven o'clock for the soul of one's late father or mother or someone else.

When they are at home, they pray five times a day. At night before dawn they drink coffee, then sleep a little and get up at dawn. They wash, drink some more coffee, and then pray the *saba*. They pray again at midday, and when *ićindia* comes, they take warm water and perform *abdes*: i.e. they wash their shaved heads, neck, nose, ears, legs up to the knees and arms up to the elbow. During their ablutions they pray to God, murmuring: '*Evšeduh Alah, ilalah, evšeduh Muhammade nasurlah*', etc. In the evening they pray the *akšam*, and two hours later they pray again the *jacia*.

If they have the misfortune to brush against pork, if only with the hem of their coat, on that day they are not allowed to pray; but for this they have the *amandžik* beside the stove, in which to wash themselves. On the following day at seven o'clock they begin to pray again, and so the dear Allah forgives them.

I have heard simple Turks say that a pig once rubbed himself against Muhammad's mosque, and that even they could eat that part of it without sinning, but they did not know which part it was. But Christians tell them it is easy to guess the part, because a pig always scratches its tail, so that if this had ever happened the pig must have rubbed its tail against the mosque.

If they have congress with a woman, whether it be their own wife or another's, they are not allowed to pray until they have washed.

It is permissible to pray anywhere and in any place. If someone wishes to pray, he must first spread something on the ground. If he has nothing, he takes off his robe and throws it onto the ground. Then, turning towards the meridian (though they themselves do not know why they turn towards the meridian, but just as Asians turn towards the meridian, so too do Bosniaks, even though for them Mecca and Medina lie not on the meridian but halfway between due east and the meridian), they raise their hands and then place their thumbs behind their ears with the fingers stretched out, just as our children do when they want to indicate big ears to someone. Then they start to pray a bit in Arabic. Next they bring their hands in front of their eyes and hold their open palms before their eyes as if reading from a book. Then they bend forward, place their hands on their knees, and murmur to themselves. Then they straighten up again, cross their arms and grasp their shoulders, murmur for a moment in this position, then bow their heads first forward, then to the left and to the right. Again they bend forward and place their hands on their knees, then kneel down and bow their heads to the ground, after which they sit for a moment on their heels, murmuring all the while. They rise again, stoop down a little, placing their hands on their knees, bring their palms once more before their eyes and, after thus reading a little, draw their palms down across their cheeks as if they were washing, which signals the end.

The simplest Turks do not themselves know how to pray, and have to seek someone who does know, praying with him as if he were a *hodža*. The person who leads the prayers is not permitted simply to murmur, but has to recite aloud, while those behind him, paying no attention to either his words or his pronunciation, merely whisper: '*Amin, Amin!*'

When the *hodža* recites the *saba,* or at any other time that pleases him, he raises his right hand with outstretched fingers against his cheek and holds it against his eye – as a harness-maker does with a horse, so that he will not be afraid – while placing his thumb on his Adam's apple. As he chants, he moves his thumb over his Adam's apple as if over some instrument, thus: 'Ićberila-a-a Alah-ila-la-a-a-a', etc.

When I was in the Serbian *kontumac,* I met there a young merchant from Macedonia who spoke three languages very well: ours, Turkish and Greek. Since he had grown up among Turks, he knew by heart all the prayers chanted by the *hodže.* To pass the time we used to tell all manner of jokes. But every time the moment came to call to prayer, he would emerge in front of our hut and call out like a *hodža.* Two days later some Bosniak Turks arrived at the *kontumac,* among them a real *hodža.* Now the two *hodže,* ours and the Turkish one, would call out together. As it happens, a Turkish letter came to the *kontumac,* which the authorities could not read, so they gave it to the Turkish *hodža* to read. The poor *hodža* burst into a sweat but was unable to read it. He finally said that he was not good at reading, but that in another hut there was a better *hodža,* who as he could tell from his voice was more learned than he: they should go and see whether he would be able to read their letter. When the Turks later learned that we did not in fact harbour a *hodža,* they were very angry. If this had happened on the Bosnian side, however, rather than being angry they would simply have cut his throat.

The Christians and the Turks hate each other a great deal. This would not be so bad if only the Christians of the two confessions got on better with each other. But although they are brethren by blood and the holy faith, they nevertheless hate each other as if they had nothing in common. The Turks call every Christian a Vlach, while the Vlachs call each other either *Šokac* or *Šiak*, though they should know that they will enjoy no happiness or progress until these shameful names are put aside.

The Turk is in general very devout in the manner of his faith: he would not break the rules, or rather I should say the rituals, of his religion (such as fasting, praying, the *sevap*, the *abdes* and washing in general) at any price. Once he has done whatever is prescribed, his heart finally grows calm and he feels as if he were reborn. The Turks are immensely proud, and feel greatly superior because dear Allah has graced them with being born in the pure faith of Muhammad. They hate terribly every infidel who refuses to acknowledge the true faith. It is a great oath for them to say: 'May I be a Vlach if ...' or, if there is a Christian present, 'May I cross myself like him if ...' I often served them instead of a *ćitap* (holy book), because I was the only Christian among them. But their oath or pledge that is supposed to last can easily be broken, if only they see some profit in it. They can say they were mistaken, because they knew not what God would ordain. One can rely more on oaths made on holy days, however, because there is no exception that would exempt them from the sin.

The common people are greatly subject to their rulers' commands. Indeed, they are ready not only to obey their commands, but also to fulfil every wish that the ruler makes known to them, however reprehensible or godless a deed it may be. They are happy only when they can fulfil their ruler's wish. The *hodža* teaches them from the Qur'an that they must not resist the smallest of their ruler's wishes. They say, therefore, that when the emperor [sultan] slew several thousand Janissaries in Istanbul, all he needed to do was to issue a *ferman* for the whole empire, stating that any Janissary might freely be killed, wherever he might be found. The Turks could hardly wait, and killed whenever and wherever they could. Several hundred people died then on both sides in Sarajevo. Only one Janissary remained at the time in Belgrade, and when they went for him the poor man tried to run away, but the Turks shut the town gates and all Belgrade grew as excited as if faced with 5,000 Janissaries. When he came running with a knife in his hand to the Stambol-kapia and saw that the gate was closed, the poor devil rushed down to Dorćul aiming for the Vidin-kapia, but the Turks fired at him from their rifles there at Dorćul and he fell dead. This happens too with lesser rulers: it is enough, for example, for a pasha or *kadia* to say before the common people that someone deserves to be killed, and they will soon bring him his head.

They are very gullible and generous when not provoked, but you have to praise them as much as you can and do them honour in the Turkish manner at the same time. The more you praise them, the prouder they are and the more they like you – they fail to grasp that what you say may not be true. So you may deceive them as much as you like, but it is wise never to violate their honour. When some misfortune occurs, they are charitable to everyone, of whatsoever faith, but they do not do it for humanity's sake – what makes them happy is that they have had an opportunity to perform *sevap* [charitable duty]. If, however, God forbid, they should get angry, there is no way under the sun that you will calm them down until they have taken your life.

They always complain about there being no war, and that they are fighting neither Vlach nor Kaurin. They never do any work, apart from artisans plying their trade or merchants seeking their profit. The others wail and lament, asking what the point of living is without a war anywhere.

Turks are very superstitious. They are all practically buried alive, as I shall show later when describing their customs. For they do not find it strange that a corpse in the grave should twitch and mumble. The poor devil, on the other hand, would jump out and refuse to be buried alive, had they not bound him head and foot and stuffed his mouth with cotton wool.

They believe in everything which for us is the subject of tongue-in-cheek stories – witches, vampires, werewolves, *vidovine*,[1] and devils who carry people off in their sleep and then bring them back. All this for them is hard truth.

Their discourse is very rough, offensive to the ear, unashamed and quite rude. God forbid that it should be taken seriously, since to do so would be a great affront to human reason. All the people of Bosnia (wherever I went) were infested with this accursed spirit, which will survive even 300 years after the Turks have gone: this is their greatest pastime, their sole education and learning about the world and mankind. Even the smallest children copy their example: having seen their worthy elders speak in such fashion, they try to behave in the same way. Some

---

1.   *Vidovine* [clairvoyants] are real people like the despot Vuk Jajčanin or Djerzelez-aga, who fought each other all the time. Vuk Jajčanin once set fire to Sarajevo, but was later killed by Djerzelez. But there were many heroes who were clairvoyant.

Christian elders try vainly to wean their young people from such Turkish language, stressing above all the infringement of God's commandments and the injury to human reason. But this does not get them very far, since the Christian youth has become almost as ill-mannered as the Turkish. If this continues much longer, it will become impossible to differentiate Turks from Christians on the basis of their discourse.

The Turks are very greedy when it comes to treasure, and seek in every way to appropriate it, whether by heroic deed, by murder or finally by cunning, when they come across it. This is why one will frequently kill another in some solitary spot, then take his treasure, fill his *ćemer* [money belt] and gird it round himself. Afterwards he will not use this money, but will simply feel happy to carry it about in his *ćemer*, until someone notices him and kills him as he had the other. Gold thus moves from one *ćemer* to another without anyone using it, except the occasional *aga* or merchant. The dervishes too behave like this: they show no qualm about killing a Christian who is not as strong as them. Merchants when travelling must take great care to avoid them, especially those who travel alone. If, however, a dervish sees that he cannot harm a Christian, he will pronounce a curse over him in the Arabic language. The dervishes are all dark-haired and originate in Arabia: few of them can say a word or two in our language, and those mispronounced. A dervish carries no other weapon than a spear with two little hatchets attached, forming a kind of cross at the top. This makes it possible for him to use it to both pierce and cut. Dervishes are Muhammadan monks of a kind, but have no permanent abode or monastery where they may live in company, and instead wander about on their own throughout the whole Muhammadan world. Some of them are as ragged as scarecrows, others are better dressed, while still others ride horses: in other words, whosoever is better at cheating and murder fares better. It is not permitted to kill a dervish: if he attacks Christians, they may only defend themselves but not kill him. I have heard, however, that one dervish threw himself upon a man from Banja Luka with his hatchet (the Bosniaks normally call the spear a hatchet), aiming to pierce him with the point sticking out from between the two little hatchets like a bayonet; but, striking only his arms-belt, he failed even to pierce the belt. The man from Banja Luka then drew his pistol, hit the dervish in the heart, and found upon him 300 golden ducats. He then dragged him to a gully beside the road, covered the blood with dry leaves, and sent his horse to roam free.

Everyone dresses in the Turkish manner. Turks tend to wear red robes, variously embroidered. Their garments are very costly, in part because they are extremely voluminous and in part because they are embroidered with gold and every kind of braid. Handsome garments, handsome weapons and a handsome chibouk is all that they care about. But this beautiful array is often covered with crawling lice. Turks refuse to kill lice, because that is *jazuk*: they are the souls of dead men who behaved villainously when they were alive, so dear Allah turned them into lice after they died. I would tell them we had no lice, but they would shout at me in unison: 'You lie like a dog: where there are people, there must also be lice!' When they see a louse crawling on the outside of their garments, they take it in their fingers and cast it on the rug beside them, so that the poor creature has to weary itself climbing back onto them; this, however, gives it a better appetite. That hellish abomination devoured me to the bone: I could scarcely get rid of it when I arrived at the Serbian *kontumac*. Christians must wear black dress made in the Turkish style if they are merchants, and on their head a *šubara* (black fur cap). They are not allowed to carry weapons in town, but only when travelling.

When I came to Sarajevo they made fun of me, saying that I had long legs like a stork, and that I was sawn apart between my legs into two poles. They told me that my dress was made of good cloth, but ruined by its poor cut. Although all *age* and *spahie* own French dress for special occasions, they nevertheless laughed a good deal at my supposedly ugly clothes, saying: 'Throw away that devil from your back! We'd never wear anything like that if we didn't have to, but no one forces you to do so.'

When Turkish women attend the mosque, they put on a long dress similar to the cassock or habit of monks, and place a *šamia* – a kind of large scarf – over their heads, which they wrap about their faces and pin together beneath their chins. The scarf forms a sort of little porch over their eyes, from beneath which if they hold their heads straight they cannot see far. This is why they usually carry their heads tilted too far back. When they go to fetch water or visit the neighbours, they do not wear the habit, but only *dimie* and a *škurteljka* [embroidered blouse], and cover their heads with a small *šamia* the end of which they hold in their teeth. If there is mud, the women wear wooden slippers on their bare feet which they call *naluhne*. The girls remain uncovered as long as they have an older unmarried sister. It was these Turkish girls who poked most fun at me, saying: 'There goes the *Švaba*! There goes the *Švaba*! He looks so funny, just like a stork.' Another would say: 'Look, sister, look at that *Kaurin*! What, would you marry him with those skinny legs of his?' One said: '*Valah*, I would indeed marry him if he were a *sendjilia* (rich man).' The others shrieked: 'But he's a Vlach, stupid!' She replied: 'Never mind that, for he'd soon convert.' For my part, I pretended not to understand, for if a Vlach exchanges one word with a Turkish girl he gets beaten on the soles of his feet.

Christian women and girls likewise always wear *dimie*, and on their heads a little red cap; around that a small *šamia* is wound, and around the *šamia* their hair is pinned. Girls do not wear the *šamia*: some pin their hair to their caps, others let it hang down.

When Turks walk through the town, they bow their heads and look down. They take long steps while keeping their legs well apart, because of the great pleat on their *čakšire* [trousers], and especially because of their *šalvale* [baggy trousers], which are 2 ells wide while the pleat hangs down to the ground. When it is muddy they hold this up with their hand. I was eager to see the outsides of the houses, so could not keep my head lowered. I was therefore constantly being cursed by the Turks, who would tell me: 'Why do you hold your head up like a *ker* [dog], and look around as if you were searching for a rotting carcass? Can't you walk with your head bowed, like a man?' Others, on the other hand, would advise me that it was a great affront to the person whose house was looked at, because people would immediately say that the viewer was on the lookout for his wives, and if the householder saw him he could kill him on the spot.

They are forever smoking a chibouk, except in front of their seniors. Especially across the pasha's *megdan* (square) it is not permitted to ride a horse or carry a chibouk; everyone has to dismount and lead his horse, and hide the chibouk somewhere on his person. Anyone appearing before the pasha who has a watch must hide its chain, so that it cannot be seen that he is wearing a watch, otherwise the pasha would punish him with beatings on the soles of his feet. The pasha, on the other hand, carries a watch in each of his pockets. Only the pasha is allowed to have an umbrella, which they call an *omrela*.

When a Turk rides across a field, no Christian is allowed to cross his path. If a Christian espies a Turk, he must give him a wide berth. This custom is akin to us doffing our hat to a superior; but whereas in our parts a superior would not beat us for failing to doff our hat to him, if ever a Turk suddenly comes across a Christian he will immediately draw his knife from his belt. When I went with the pasha to Travnik, there was thick snow with a path trodden into it. We frequently met *kiridžie* with their loads, who, having no space into which they might divert their horses, would simply run away to the woods leaving their horses on the path. The angry Turks, left with no one to beat, would jump down from their own horses and push the horses of the *kiridžije* into the snow, thus opening the way forward. After we had gone far ahead, we could see the poor people struggling with their horses. Once we met some *kiridžie* on a steep bank: the Turks pushed the horses so far away from the road that the unfortunate animals rolled down the slope, loads and all, until they came to a halt somewhere in the snow. And when the people returned, they wailed over them.

When Turks wish to eat, they set a *sofra* [low table] in the middle of the room and sit around it cross-legged. If soup is served, they take out spoons from their belts, while anybody not carrying one on his belt is given his at the *sofra*. After finishing the soup, they set the spoons aside and eat the rest of the food with their fingers. If the food is greasy, pieces of bread are broken off and used for scooping from the *sahan* [dish]. One is not allowed to cut bread with a knife, because that is *jazuk*. When meat arrives, pieces are torn off by hand, in order of age. If any liquid from some dish remains at the bottom of the *sahan*, the elders get to drink it first, but if none wants it the youngest may have it. If there is plenty of liquid, the elders drink first then give it to the younger and so on. Since knives are not permitted at table, common folk gnaw at the bones with their teeth, while gentlefolk pick at them with their fingers and then throw them away. Yoghurt (soured milk) always comes at the end of the meal: save only that there be none. Hands are washed before meals, after the meal both hands and mouth. Many wash their mouths with soap.

The hardest thing for me was sitting at the *sofra*, because my legs would grow numb. And even if they did not grow numb, I was unable to fold my legs beneath me as they did. I was scolded for this many times: they told me that one should learn the proper manner. Though it is true that I had been born among *Švabe*, I was now among men, and should learn, therefore, how to behave properly, so that people would not make fun of me. 'It's time you forgot that cur's habit!' they would say. Others would add: 'Convert then, you fool! And God will give you *selamet* [salvation]. You'll be covered in rich gold and purple and your soul will go to *dženet*. If you don't convert, poor man, you'll burn for ever in *dženam* or *džan* as if in this *furuna* (oven).' Some would ask me why our priest bends three times over the child he is christening. 'I don't know,' I said. 'No one has ever told me.' They replied: 'If you don't know, we'll tell you. When the priest is christening a child he bends over him three times saying: "Convert, foolish child! Convert, foolish child! Convert, foolish child, so that you don't blame me in the other world." You, however, think that he's giving him God knows what blessing.'

Practically every house, or every better-off one, has a large trough the size of a man, and a large *kazan* (pot) for heating water. When someone falls gravely ill, they watch him so that he does not die without them noticing. As soon as the sick man stops breathing, they start to shout at each other as if they were in fear: 'Quickly, go to the *kazan*, light the fire and heat the water before his body gets cold,' for it would be a great sin for the body to cool down before they have washed it. They say that the saint will not come to the dead man until he has been washed. Once they have washed him, they stuff his nose, mouth, ears and all his bodily orifices with cotton wool, and wrap him up in a new sheet from the soles of his feet to the top of his head, like a small baby. By the time they have performed this important task, others will have dug his grave. All the family and friends now gather together, one of whom must be a *hodža*. They place his body in a simple box, which at the bottom has two strips of wood nailed to it, rather like the axles on a cart. The people attending the funeral pair off in front of his house, and when the dead man is brought out those who are closest to the door lift him onto their shoulders, then, keeping him no longer than it takes to utter a sound, they pass him along to the shoulders of those next to them; these, after holding him for a moment, pass him on to others. In this way he is passed on from one to another, while those who are left behind rush forward and wait for their turn to come again. In this way, from shoulder to shoulder, they bring him to the graveyard, where they take him out of the box and lay him wrapped up as he is in the grave, upon the bare earth. They cover him over with thick planks, and scatter some earth over the planks. They tell me that on several occasions, after lowering the dead man into the grave, he would start to twitch, and to mumble like this: hm, hm, hm. Then they would all start to run away, while the *hodža* would say to him: '*Korkma, korkma, korkmago!*' If it happens that a dead man begins twitching and mumbling before the grave is covered over with the planks, and all flee in panic, the *hodža* himself must not run away but himself close the grave, all the while comforting the man: '*Korkma, korkma!*' On such occasions, when the *hodža* decides to go home he must walk backwards, shouting all the while: '*Korkma! Korkmago!*' I asked them what *korkma* meant, and what the cause was for the dead body twitching. They told me the following: '*Korkma* means: do not be afraid. You ask how a dead body can twitch? We know very well that a Vlach will never twitch, because the *šejtan* takes him off to *džan*; but when a righteous Turk dies and is placed in the grave, a saint comes to him and, after conversing with him, takes him to *dženet.*'

Adultery is the worst sin among Turks. If a Turk visits the wife of another Turk and is caught for the third time, he is impaled. If a Christian man visits a Turkish woman who has no husband, the first time he is caught he must either convert and marry her or he will be impaled. If the Turkish woman is married already, however, the adulterer without exception is impaled. If a Christian man visits a married Christian woman and is caught, he is promptly hanged. A Turk, on the other hand, may visit a Christian woman without any fear of punishment.

No one in Bosnia owns their land: the pasha can take everything from one person and give it to another. This is why the larger farmers, especially those who are Christian, must – in accordance with their possibilities – bribe the pasha, pretending to be his friends. When the pasha wishes to fine someone, he demands from him a loan of five, six or ten purses, whatever he wants. If he refuses to loan the money the pasha pretends to be angry and has him executed as a rebel, after which he appropriates his property quite publicly. Those who do lend him money are immediately given a date by which he will return it. When the date draws near, the pasha sends *kavaze* to fetch such and such a merchant (his creditor) to him in bonds. The *kavazi* go and do as the worthy pasha bids them. When the bound merchant comes before the pasha, he is as fearful as a slave: he knows well that no lavishness awaits him. As soon as the pasha sees him, he cries out: 'You wretch, how dared you do such and such?' He invents something, or charges him on the spot: with having carried some *espape* [merchandise] without paying the *djurmuk*; or with having sworn at a Turk; or if nothing else, he accuses him of having boasted to some people about how he had lent the pasha so many purses. Wishing to vindicate himself, the merchant says typically: 'I didn't do it, honourable pasha; someone has maliciously lied about me.' The pasha flares up at these words and shouts: 'What, sirrah cross, you mean that

I'm lying? Take him away, men, and give him a hundred on the soles of his feet!' The merchant starts to beg: 'Don't, honourable pasha, don't, for your child's sake. Please forgive me if I have offended you; I will pay whatever you want.' The *kavazi* then take hold of him like devils seizing a sinful soul and drag him into the courtyard. The pasha now pretends to have taken pity, and says: 'Don't, boys, stop! It's mercy for him this first time. Let him now pay the fine, but it must not happen again.' He then says to the prisoner: 'You, Moskov,[1] you'll pay so many purses for your offence. As for insulting me, I'll forgive you this time, but you should watch out in future. You've lent me so many purses, and now you need to give me so many more.' The merchant is then forced to lay out more purses as the pasha demands. The Christians know this custom well: that if they give, they are more likely to get beatings than their money back; and if they don't, they will lose both their property and their life. This is why, when they lend him money and he starts to accuse them falsely, they at once beg him, saying that they will pay whatever he decides to be right. When I accompanied them to Travnik, the pasha, not wishing to spend his money, borrowed sixty purses from Christian merchants and thirty purses from Jewish ones.

Any man is allowed to kill his wife when he wishes, and any master his servant, for the smallest infringement, especially if he is Christian. This is why, when a foreigner appears before an *aga*, *kadia* or some other notable, the courtiers must say in the

---

1.   Ever since the Bosniaks fought the Russians at Istanbul and many became Russian prisoners of war, the word Moscow has remained embedded in their minds. This is why Bosnian gentlefolk when angry will call a Christian 'Moskov', meaning someone who is stubborn, disobedient, arrogant or insubordinate.

presence of his master and the whole gathering: 'Our *aga* (or whatever his title may be) may kill all of us here.' This implies that he can kill the foreigner too. The *aga* then sagely lifts his head and says: 'But no, God forbid, I will not touch honest people.' The courtiers repeat: 'He may take everything from us, and imprison or kill us all, whenever he wants!' The *aga* again shakes his head, strokes his beard and says: 'Ah, no! Never fear! I won't, no, I won't do that. *Aja ćs*,[1] I won't do it.' While they praise him in this way, the foreigner who does not know the local custom must feel his hair stand on end.

The bodies of executed men are not buried, but rather thrown onto the rubbish heap as *sevap* to feed the dogs.

Deserters from the Austrian army who have fled to Bosnia are today the most wretched slaves. As soon as a fugitive arrives, the first *kadia* who catches him makes him his slave. He must do what the *kadia* commands, and the *kadia* may sell him or execute him at will. An infantryman and a cavalryman shed bitter tears in front of me, saying: 'If we could only return to the bliss in which we dwelt in Germany, we should think we'd arrived in paradise! Do you see, dear brother, our torn clothes? They are given to us by our master, who in addition feeds us miserably. We have had no money in our hands for years!' The Turks questioned me too about whether I might not be a fugitive. 'Ahaa!' I said. 'Fugitives do not bear such passports, just look at the quality of its seal.' '*Valaha*, it's true, read us something from it.' I read it out to them, incurring no danger since they understood nothing.

---

1. The word *ćs* signals negation, as in our parts. To pronounce it, the tongue must be firmly attached to the palate next to the upper teeth and, having drawn in breath, you release it suddenly to make the sound *ćs*. I do not know how to write it down differently.

If I had said I was a fugitive, however, not even nine passports would have set me free.

The Turks keep many dogs of one particular breed. They are large, long and thin, but friendly, and they lie about in the streets as though dead. There are more of them than there are sheep, and when one walks along the street one must circle around so as not step on them or trip over them. To hit one would incur a strong reaction from the Turks. Turks do not bury carcasses or dead animals, but throw them into the street for the dogs to feed on them. They say that the more dogs they feed, the greater is their *sevap*.

I asked them in particular why Turks do not drink wine. They said: Because wine is God's blood. But don't worry, they would gladly drink it were they not scared that God might suddenly throw them into the abyss, where they will later go anyway.

Each winter the Bosnian Turks threaten that when spring comes they will go to liberate Šumadia and divide it into spahiluks: this for them is liberation. Whenever someone mentions Šumadia, the others immediately say: 'Just you wait! In the spring, God willing!' And when a Turkish merchant returns from Serbia, everyone asks him: 'Do tell us, do, how are things in Šumadia? How do our brothers Turks fare there? Are they left in peace? Are they tried in Vlach courts? Do they wear a *pusad* [arms-belt]? Or pay taxes to the Vlachs?' They reply: '*Valaha* and by my faith, our pure faith has been ruined there. Our people have shut themselves up in the fortresses. But what can they eat in the forts? They must go to the countryside, and the countryside all belongs to the Vlachs. When we get there, no one displays any liking for us. They all look unfriendly, and for whatever we buy we must pay more than a Vlach. If someone gives you food or drink, you must pay for all of it: a Vlach will not even walk your horse for nothing. They have plenty of everything, but won't let you have it. Šumadia has never been so rich as it is now: wherever you look it is like Egypt. Yet they will not give you a light for your pipe unless you pay for it. They think that we have plenty of gold and silver, not knowing that we go hungry and thirsty in their land. There is nothing else to do but arise and go to liberate our brothers and spread our pure faith.' The others try to comfort them, saying: 'Never mind! In the spring, God willing.'

The Turks say that they are the best-looking and the noblest nation in the world in regard to both faith and blood; and that all *kaur* kings[1] would like to have their species of man. They cite as evidence of this many such requests on the part of *kaur* kings. One of them said this, among other things: 'I once attended a meeting in Kostajnica. A *kaur* general, which is something like our vizier, arrived and from the start kept looking across at our side. We watched him too. He asked me in particular, since I was sitting a little apart, to come nearer so that we might talk. I drew closer to him, whereupon he asked me if I would come over to their side. I asked: "And what would I do on your side?" He replied: "You will have nice clothes, comfortable lodgings, good food, and everything you need, as well as three thousand groschen per month."'

---

1. One must not say in Bosnia to the Turks that we too have an emperor. They say that there can be only one emperor in the world and he is their own in Istanbul. The Kaurin have only seven kings. The Christians, on the other hand, say that there are only two emperors, the Russian and the Turkish, one German Kaiser and seven other kings.

They say that everywhere across the Kaur lands stakes are implanted on the mountains and hills and a tar beacon tied to each. A watchtower stands next to each stake. So the *Švabe* are on one side of the cordon and our Turks on the other. But whereas a Turk is not permitted to do anything to a *Švaba*, the *Švaba* will keep provoking from the other side, cursing the Turk's wife or sister or honour.[1] Should our man utter so much as a word, however, the *Švaba* on the other side will immediately fire his gun. If our Turks rush up and kill even a single *Švaba*, the nearest watchtower will quickly light its beacon. As soon as the flame is seen, all the other watchtowers light their beacons. Within half an hour all seven *kaur* kings know accordingly that it is war against the Turk. If one did not try to calm matters down promptly, they would invade from all sides.

They say that books from all over the world can be found in the Kaur lands, recording everything that has ever happened, and that here especially the German keeps a full record of how many times he has waged war against the Turk, and how many people were killed. And the German, they say, writes it all down properly: if the Turk was stronger, then it's the Turk; if the German, then it's the German. He makes no distinction. Others ask: 'But why, may God destroy him?' Others again reply: 'Eh, my brother, because he wants it to be known. Do you really reckon that it's like when we play the *gusle* and sing about killing the Vlachs, as if Vlach heads were like cabbages?' Yet another joins in: 'Yes, by my faith, and who was Prince Marko? And what about Vuk of Jajce? Miloš Obilić, who was particularly

---

1. The greatest offence to the Turk is to swear at his wife or sister or honour; one such word is enough for one to kill another. They do not react so strongly if someone curses his mother or something else of his.

strong, swore that he would crush the neck of the emperor at Kosovo and eat part of him with bacon. And indeed, *efendum benum*,[1] he did mount his horse and go to Kosovo. The whole army had to make way for him, and he entered the emperor's tent. No sooner had he entered the tent than he at once slit the emperor apart with his knife. Then, however, he forgot what he had said about eating part of the sultan with bacon, but he drew out his sabre and instead proceeded to rout the emperor's entire army single-handed. He killed there, *džanum* [dear soul], eighty thousand soldiers. And when he finally reached the end of the field, he remembered that he had not fulfilled his pledge, so he returned to the emperor's tent, placed his foot on his neck, and ate part of him with bacon. Before Miloš had finished, a Vlach *baba* came along, who was a witch, and instructed the few remaining Turks who had managed to save themselves with their beg how to catch Miloš alive. They did what the *baba* told them: around the tent they planted all the spears upside down. When Miloš, having fulfilled his pledge, came riding out of the tent, his horse was impaled on the spears, and Miloš tumbled down. The Turks rushed up and bound his hands behind his back. Miloš was surprised, lad, how it had come about that the Turks were so clever. They told him that it was not their idea, but that the *baba* had taught them. He begged them before killing him to bring the *baba* to him, supposedly just in order to take a look at her. When our Turks, *efendum benum*, brought the *baba*, Miloš approached her with his hands tied as if he wished

---

1. When the Turks tell tales they sit cross-legged, hold the big toe of their right foot with the forefinger of their left hand and with their right hand stroke their beards repeatedly, especially when they say '*efendum benum*' – even if they don't have a beard, they keep stroking their chins.

to tell her something; then he turned his back on her, caught her nose with the middle fingers of his right hand as if with pincers, twirled her once around him, and threw her right across Kosovo. Although she was an old witch, her bones nevertheless fell apart and she promptly died. Our people, seeing his strength, quickly cut him down, because, *džanum*, he might have tossed one of them like that.'

But there is another thing that weighs upon my heart, which I will register here so that I may feel a little better. No Christian youth can visit the *čaršija* except on business. This is because, when a Turk buys something at the *čaršija*, he looks out to see if he may spot some unoccupied Vlach. And if there is none, he takes one going about his own business and tells him: 'Here, young man, carry this for me.' The man, who might have nine major errands, must leave them all and serve the Turk. When an unidentified Christian passes through some other village, the Turks persuade their children (which is not very difficult, given their nature) to throw mud and stones at him, and to ask him for money. The children will not let go of him until he pays them off. This happened to me on two occasions. Once in Travnik I had taken a walk round the *čaršija* when, on my return, children accosted me from all sides, shouting: 'There goes a cross! Hit him! Give us money, sirrah lime-wood cross! Redeem yourself.' Luckily it was snowing, so they had nothing to throw at me apart from snowballs. An *aga* from Travnik happened to come by and he drove the children away, so I did not have to pay the ransom. Another time, when I was leaving Sarajevo, as I have already said I was accompanied by Omer-čauš to the lower gates of the fortress. I traversed the fortress on my own, or rather not on my own, but in the company of children. The snow had in the meantime started to melt, especially along the paths trodden by people, so my retinue had plenty of mud and stones to do me the honours. I refused to give them any money, hoping that some good man would once again come by and free me. But when one child hit me in the face so that mud covered my right eye, my heart boiled up and I threw the cudgel I was carrying at them. Luckily I did not hit any of them. The Turks, who up to then had cared nothing for me, now seized me and took me to the *dizdar*. When the *dizdar* had read through my passport, however, and seen that I had been with the pasha, he let me go and told the others that no one was to touch me.

Since I have said much about Bosnia, it would be right to say a few words about Serbia, but space does not permit it. I will say briefly only what fits in well here. Serbia is very beautiful in regard to its natural position. Most of it is covered in magnificent forests, which is why the Turks call it Šumadia [*šuma* = a forest]. For Serbia insists that there should be no Turks in it, but only Serbs, which maddens the Turks. Serbia is in the grip of a mighty fighting spirit, as our saying goes: 'The old man tells tales of battle and land, and the young man next to him blazes like a hearth.' That is what present-day Serbia is like. Soldiers from Kara-Djordje's day tell tales about how they killed Turks, how the Turks persecuted them, how they liberated themselves, how many of them perished on Kamenica, at which time Kara-Djordje left Serbia and the Turkish pasha erected a tower made of Serbian heads. These words fill the young people with mighty wrath, and they show great fury also at their government which will not let them fight the Turks and revenge the tower built by the Turks at Kamenica, in the belief that they would in this way scare all Serbia. They say that the tower had four corners, and that its outer surface was imbedded with skulls. The elders, however, say that the skulls were not Serb ones alone, but both Serb and Turkish; that the Turks collected the heads of all who had died there and merely pretended that they were only Serb. The young people, on the other hand, say that one should believe what the Turks say: for the debt is paid in accordance with what the debtor himself declares.

Glossary

Some Turkish Barbarisms

Abdest, a	*m.*	ablution
Aps, a	*m.*	jail
Aferim!	*interj*.	true, true!
Aga, e	*m.*	gentleman, master
Ahar, a	*m.*	stable, stall
Ajan, a	*m.*	type of Turkish officer
Ajluk, a	*m.*	official bribe
Akšam, a	*m.*	dusk, prayer at nightfall among the Turks
Alah, a	*m.*	God
Alas, a	*m.*	1. bath
		2. faith
		3. grace, pardon, clemency
Amandžik, a	*m.*	basin beside the stove
Amanet, a	*m.*	pledge
Ašća, e	*m.*	cook
Ašikovati	*v. a.*	to go courting
Ašikmahala, e	*f.*	place for courting, for lovers

Azur	*adj.* *indecl.*	prepared, ready
Badava	*adj.*	in vain
Bajram, a	*m.*	Turkish holiday
Baka	*interj.*	look!, see!
Bakal, a	*m.*	grocer (shopkeeper)
Bakalnica, e	*f.*	grocery shop
Barabar	*adj.*	equally, directly
Bardak, a	*m.*	copper jug with handle
Baš, a	*m.*	head
	adj.	precisely, just
Baša, e	*m.*	master, used also for a master craftsman, as we say *majstor*: but in Turkish anyone engaged in a trade is a *majstor* (i.e. *usta*)
Bašća, e	*f.*	garden
Baška	*adv.*	alone, otherwise
Bat, a	*m.*	luck
Batal	*indecl.*	ruined, broken down, perhaps of local derivation
Batli	*adj.*	lucky
Batlia, e	*m.*	lucky person
Bećar, a	*m.*	unmarried man, bachelor
Beg, a	*m.*	type of high Turkish nobleman
Begenisati	*v. a.*	to choose, be enamoured, love, approve
Bekria, e	*f.*	human degenerate
Belaj, a	*m.*	woe, calamity, misfortune
Beli beli	*adj.*	indeed, indeed
Berberin, a	*m.*	barber
Berberbaša, e	*m.*	master barber
Berićat, a	*m.*	harvest, progress

Berićet oslum	*interj.*	thank you, thanks
Bešluk, a	*m.*	a five, 5 groschen
Bezbeli	*adj.*	yes, indeed, truly, surely
Bina, e	*f.*	building
Budžak, a	*m.*	corner
Bundava, e	*f.*	pumpkin, marrow
Čakšire, ah	*f. pl.*	trousers
Čardak, a	*m.*	cabin on stilts
Čaršija, e	*f.*	marketplace, market
Čaršilia, e	*m.*	market trader
Čauš, a	*m.*	a Turkish dignitary
Česma, e	*f.*	water-pipe, aqueduct
Čibuk, a	*m.*	long-stemmed pipe
Činia, e	*f.*	dish, wooden bowl
Čoha, e	*f.*	cloth
Čorba, e	*f.*	soup
Čuruk	*adj.*	rotten
Ćehaja, e	*m.*	secretary
Ćeif, a	*m.*	desire, appetite, perhaps from *htěti, htjev* [to wish, wish]
Ćemer, a	*m.*	belt, arch
Ćilim, a	*m.*	rug
Ćitap, a	*m.*	book on which oaths are sworn
Ćoso, e	*m.*	clean-shaven man
Ćošak, ška	*m.*	corner
Ćupria, e	*m.*	bridge
Drviš, a	*m.*	Muhammadan monk
Degramadžia, e	*m.*	joiner, cabinet-maker

Dekik, a	*m.*	moment, minute
Dimie, ah	*f. pl.*	baggy trousers, bloomers
Din, a	*m.*	law
Dina mi!	*interj.*	my faith!
Direk, a	*m.*	column, beam
Divanhana, e	*f.*	terrace
Dizdar, a	*m.*	commander of fortress gates (castellan)
Djaur, a	*m.*	infidel
Djumruk, a	*m.*	toll, tax (one-thirtieth)
Dolap, a	*m.*	wardrobe
Dućan, a	*m.*	shop
Dura!	*interj.*	halt!
Durbin, a	*m.*	binoculars, eyeglass
Dušek, a	*m.*	the word is ours and means *die Matratze* [mattress]
Duvar, a	*m.*	wall
Džambas, a	*m.*	trickster
Džamia, e	*f.*	Muhammadan church
Džanum	*interj.*	dear, e.g. my dear, dear soul
Dženabet, a	*m.*	rascal
Dženom, a	*m.*	Muhammadan hell
Dženet, a	*m.*	Muhammadan heaven
Džumbuš, a	*m.*	hubbub, merrymaking
Efendum benum	*interj.*	good sir!
Ejvala	*interj.*	my respects
Eglendisati	*v. a.*	to talk
Eglendžija, e	*m.*	talkative person, talker
Eksik	*adv.*	less
Esap, a	*m.*	reckoning

Esapiti	*v. a.*	to reckon
Espap, a	*m.*	goods
Ferman, a	*m.*	imperial missive
Findžan, a	*m.*	coffee cup, small cup
Furuna, e	*f.*	stove
Gajtan, a	*m.*	braid
Gazda, e	*m.*	master in general; I doubt this is Turkish
Haber, a	*m.*	message, report
Hadet, a	*m.*	custom, habit
Hajvan, a	*m.*	stock, cattle, livestock
Han, a	*m.*	stopping-place for travellers
Handžia, e	*m.*	master of a *han*
Halal	*adv.*	vulgarly
Halaliti	*v. a.*	to excuse, pardon, forgive
Halat, a	*m.*	tools
Harač, a	*m.*	capitation, poll-tax
Haram	*adj.*	proscribed
Harem, a	*m.*	women's quarters
Hasura, e	*f.*	rush mat
Hazna, e	*f.*	treasury, coffer
Helbetum	*adv.*	as if, for instance
Hič	*adv.*	nothing
Hodža, e	*m.*	Muhammadan priest
Ićindia, e	*f.*	evening prayer
Insan, a	*m.*	person
Izum, a	*m.*	permit
Jabandžia, e	*m.*	stranger, foreigner

Jacia, e	*f.*	two hours after sunset
Jastuk, a	*m.*	pillow, cushion
Jazuk, a	*m.*	fault, harm, sin
Jedek, a	*m.*	1. horse
		2. bridle
		3. pots
Jemek, a	*m.*	food, provender
Jogurt, a	*m.*	sour milk
Jok jok	*interj.*	it's not it's not, no no
Jok valah!	*interj.*	it's not by God!

Kadar	*adj.*	capable
Kadia, e	*m.*	judge, magistrate
Kadiluk, a	*m.*	judgeship, *kadia*'s jurisdiction
Kafeodžak, a	*m.*	coffee shop
Kafedžibaša, e	*m.*	master coffee-maker
Kail	*adj.*	willing
Kalp	*adj.*	bogus, false
Kapidžik, a	*m.*	little door
Kapia, e	*f.*	door
Kar, a	*m.*	violence, woe
Karaula, e	*f.*	guardhouse
Karli	*adj.*	distressed, confused, concerned, worried
Karlica, e	*f.*	wooden bowl, tight spot
Kasap, kasapin, a	*m.*	butcher
Kasapnica, e	*f.*	butcher's shop
Kašika, e	*m.*	spoon
Kaur, kaurin, a	*m.*	foreign infidel; this is how the Bosniaks understand it
Kavaz, a	*m.*	constable
Kavga, e	*f.*	trouble, quarrel

Kazan, a	*m.*	cauldron
Ker, e	*m.*	dog
Kiria, e	*f.*	hire
Kiridžia, e	*m.*	hired driver
Kolan, a	*m.*	girth
Komšia, e	*m.*	neighbour
Komšiluk, a	*m.*	neighbourhood
Konak, a	*m.*	abode, night-quarters
Korban bajram, a	*m.*	main Turkish holiday
Korkma	*interj.*	do not fear
Korkmago	*interj.*	do not fear
Kula, e	*f.*	keep, tower
Kurtalisati	*v. a.*	to rescue, redeem
Lelek, a	*m.*	stork
Magaza, e	*f.*	storehouse
Mahala, e	*f.*	part of town, village, quarter
Mahrama, e	*f.*	scarf
Mandal, a	*m.*	door-bar
Mazgala, e	*f.*	embrasure (loophole)
Maša ala	*interj.*	is shouted out, when something is praised for its beauty
Medet, a	*masc.*	Turks say this as their last word, when they are dying
Mehana, e	*f.*	inn, tavern
Mehandžia, e	*m.*	innkeeper
Mejdan, megdan, a	*m.*	open space, square
Mezil, a	*m.*	mail
Mezulhana, e	*f.*	mail station, post office

Mezuldžia, e	*m.*	mail courier
Misir, a	*m.*	Great Cairo, Egypt
More	*interj.*	term of abuse, as it were: fool, idiot
Mukaet	*adj.*	patient
Munara, e	*f.*	part of a mosque from which the *hodža* calls, tower
Muntaf, a	*m.*	horse blanket
Mur, a	*m.*	stamp for sealing, signet-ring
Murafet, a	*m.*	1. painter's implements
		2. painting
Musafer, a	*m.*	traveller
Museveda, e	*f.*	affliction, abuse
Muštuluk, a	*m.*	promised reward, sweetmeat. Gift for good tidings
Nagraisati	*v. n.*	come to grief
Nizam, a	*m.*	regular Turkish soldier
Nutvak, a	*m.*	kitchen
Odadžia, e	*m.*	valet
Odaja, e	*m.*	room
Odžak, a	*m.*	chimney, hearth
Osmanlija, e	*m.*	Bosniaks call real Turks *Osmanlije* [Ottomans]
Para, e	*f.*	Turkish coin; 20 silver kreutzers make 146 *pare*
Paša, see B[aša]		
Pashaluk, a	*m.*	district
Peke peke	*interj.*	fine, fine
Pendžer, a	*m.*	window, casement

Peškeš, a	*m.*	bribe
Pilav, a	*m.*	rice gruel
Pusat, i	*f.*	small arms
Qur'an, a	*m.*	Muhammadan holy writ
Rafa, e	*f.*	shelf, furniture
Rahat	*adj.*	favourably, with good reason, comfortably
Raja, e	*m.*	subject people
Ramazan, a	*m.*	Turkish fast
Rezil	*adj.*	wrong, bogus, false
Saba, e	*f.*	dawn
Sabile	*adv.*	at dawn
Sàhan, a	*m.*	copper dish
Saibia, e	*m.*	owner, master
Sakat	*adj.*	lame
Salam, a	*m.*	benediction and salutation
Salamet, a	*m.*	crudity, licence
Salaš, a	*m.*	harness-maker, saddler
Saračana, e	*f.*	saddle-room
Sarajlia, e	*m.*	native of Sarajevo
Senči	*adv.*	ostensibly
Sevap, a	*m.*	pious endowment
Siaset, a	*m.*	multitude, mass
Sikter bre	*interj.*	very insulting and abusive threat
Sikterisat	*v. a.*	drive away shamefully
Škurteljka, e	*f.*	woman's dress, skirt; I don't believe it is a Turkish word
Sokak, a	*m.*	street
Spahia, e	*m.*	nobleman who goes to war on his own horse, and in his own uniform

Stambol, a	*m.*	Istanbul
Sofra, e	*m.*	table half an ell wide, round, and a span high
Sunet, a	*m.*	circumcision
Sunetžia, e	*m.*	circumciser
Surudžia, e	*m.*	postal lackey
Šamia, e	*f.*	woman's head scarf
Šalvale, ah	*f. pl.*	baggy trousers
Šećer, a	*m.*	sugar
Šejtan, a	*m.*	devil, Satan, fiend
Šiša, e	*f.*	glass, bottle; God knows if it is a Turkish word!
Tain, a	*m.*	baker's bread
Taman	*adv.*	exactly, directly
Taraba, e	*f.*	thick plank, picket fence
Tatarin, a	*m.*	messenger, courier
Teferič, a	*m.*	summer residence, country outing
Teskera, e	*f.*	passport, paper; it can hardly be Turkish
Testir	*adj.*	crudely, with licence
Top, a	*m.*	bombard, gun, cannon
Topčia, e	*m.*	gunner
Turbe, eta	*m.*	memorial, gravestone in the form of a little column
Tutundžia, e	*m.*	tobacco-seller, and also young gentleman; comes from *tutun* tobacco, hence tobacconist
Ustra, e	*f.*	razor
Uzdenjia, e	*f.*	stirrup

Valah!	*interj.*	by God!
Valaha!	*interj.*	by God!
Valaha bilaha	*interj.*	Turkish oath, yes, by God!
Većil, a	*m.*	steward, regent
Većilašćia, e	*m.*	kitchen steward
Vilaet, a	*m.*	province, world, state
Vlah, a	*m.*	what Turks maliciously call Christians
Zanat, a	*m.*	handicraft, this may come from our *znati* [to know]
Zanatdžia, e	*m.*	craftsman, artisan
Ziafet, a	*m.*	display of respect, honour
Zian, a	*m.*	derision, shame, reproof
Zor, a	*m.*	impetus, force
Zorile	*adv.*	forcibly, strongly, robustly
Zulum, a	*m.*	violence, cruelty
Zulumčar, a	*m.*	cruel, violent, bloodthirsty person, tyrant, cut-throat

About the Author

The roots of the Mažuranić family lie deep in the past and are so much wrapped in legend that, despite the fact that the family had long recorded their history, it is difficult to establish reliable facts. Even their contemporaries felt that the biographies of some members of the Mažuranić family read like a fable. This is true especially for Matija Mažuranić and his son Fran, whose adventurous lives have an almost literary quality.

The heroic *uskok* tradition of service on the border, and the national spirit of Kačić's poetry, were appreciated early on and nursed in the family, which 'enhanced the aura of the Mažuranić name'. But no branch of the Mažuranić family's profuse tree has given so many illustrious names to Croatia's cultural history as that of the judge from Novi, Ivan, which produced three brothers: Ivan, the poet and ban of Croatia, author of the epic *The Death of Smail-aga Čengijić*; Antun, the philologist; and Matija, author of the work of travel literature *A Glance into Ottoman Bosnia*. Their descendants too have made major contributions to Croatian literature: Matija's son Fran

Mažuranić is the author of a small but marvellous collection of verses, *Leaves*; and Ivan's granddaughter Ivana Brlić-Mažuranić became a celebrated writer of books for children. One could add to this list Matija's grandson Milutin Mažuranić, and Ivan's great-grandson Ivan Brlić, for their contributions to the biographies of many members of the Mažuranić family, in particular those of Ivan and Matija.

Matija was born on 4 February 1817 in Novi Vinodolski. He attended a German-language primary school, but he was the youngest son and there was not enough money for his further education, so he became a blacksmith. His inquiring mind and natural talent led Matija, however, to browse through his elder brothers' school textbooks. On reaching maturity he became a builder, and studied applied science in Vienna as a part-time student. He spent the best part of his life running a construction firm and building roads in the [Croatian] Littoral and the Military Border. Being of restless spirit, he frequently went abroad, sometimes for several years. He travelled to Bosnia several times, and to Istanbul, Asia Minor, Mesopotamia, Egypt, and all over Austria. In Turkey he acquired a considerable reputation as well as considerable wealth. Having learned to speak Turkish well during his first journey to Bosnia, during his stay in Istanbul he was named Croat-pasha and appointed honorary magistrate in cases involving our people. Full of adventure too was the part of his life he spent in Croatia, building roads in the border in between his travels and seeking to outwit the hajduks of Krbava, Ogulin and Zrmanja.

He died, mentally ill, on 17 April 1881 in a hospital in Graz, aged sixty-four. He left behind only one written work, *A*

Glance into Ottoman Bosnia, the first travel book of Croatia's modern period, written in an exceptionally fine prose of the Illyrian period.

***

Matija was only twenty-two when his brothers, the well-known Illyrians Ivan and Antun, sent him to Bosnia to ascertain the state of national awareness among the Bosnian people, because at that time, in the 1830s, there were many rumours of repression and tough political conditions, as well as of rebellions against the Turkish government. This is how Matija's grandson, Milutin Mažuranić, presents the matter in his biographical essay 'Matija Mažuranić, brother of the poet and ban':

> In the absence of contacts with those parts, it was necessary to go there oneself. This is why in 1839 the two Mažuranić brothers sent their own Matija over there, to get in touch with the Muslims and to find out whether something could be done for the realisation of their aspirations. Such a thing could be attempted only in secret, and there was no one better qualified for it than Matija, who in addition to all his other merits knew two trades and could fit in anywhere.
>
> Matija fulfilled his task most excellently. Having avoided several near catastrophes, he did so well that he even succeeded (though a Christian) in changing from a 'servitor' into a friend of, and trusted adviser

to, a number of Muslim leaders. He also mastered the Turkish language, which even many Bosnian begs could not speak.

Returning a year later to Zagreb, he submitted a written report to his brothers, which suggested that the Muslim movement did not amount to anything much, because it was more religious than political in nature, although the Bosnian begs were deep down pretty nationally minded and desirous of freedom. The people were not awakened, or ready for battle; but a general uprising was nevertheless in the making and might indeed break out at any time, because the people had had enough. Antun and Ivan, having read his report and being impressed by their brother's intelligent and farsighted perception, as well as the harmoniousness and purity of his language, tried to persuade him to write up for publication something about his travels. He agreed and wrote *A Glance into Ottoman Bosnia*. After the three brothers, working together, had eliminated everything of a political nature or that might harm anyone, the small book came out anonymously in 1842, although it was known – even in the Czech lands – who had written it.

Bosnia at that time, although next door, was a distant, exotic and dangerous land, and above all quite unknown. As the author writes in his introduction, 'we have learnt to know the Germans, the Italians, the French and the English better than ourselves'.

His work fully realised its intention. So much that was new

and interesting was condensed in it within a relatively small space that it could not fail to cause a sensation. The author portrayed both Christians and Muslims, their public and private life, their customs, their sanitary conditions, their houses and squares, their animals, the rich and the poor. The relationship between the common people and their masters, which Ivan Mažuranić would subsequently evoke in *The Death of Smail-Aga Čengijić*, and Utješenović and Martić in their poems, Matija Mažuranić showed in a documentary, direct and moving fashion.

This was the national significance of *A Glance into Ottoman Bosnia*. But the work also has a remarkable literary quality, embedded in the author's personal and creative nature, the vivacity of his portrayals and its expressive power.

Matija Mažuranić, adventurous and full of pluck, describes in his small book a series of reckless deeds that only a man attracted by danger could have accomplished. Examples of such adventures are his first attempt to smuggle himself across the Sava into Bosnia, or his crossing to Belgrade in a leaky boat. Everywhere, on each page, the author's restless spirit breaks out.

A Glance into Ottoman Bosnia keeps one spellbound from start to finish. Its writer, unspoiled by foreign travelogues, brings out true events. He watched and studied people and their ways of life, and he expressed this in the language used by unaffected and sensible people untainted by bookish sapience. He supplied a wealth of details that many scholars would either fail to notice or not know how to read. He had, in addition, a strong talent for story-telling. His travelogue flows from beginning to end like a story, with some parts being highlighted like anecdotes.

Matija Mažuranić's style displays density and precision. Rendering faithfully the events in which he took part, he tells a simple tale without seeking to dramatise. It is precisely because he uses so few words to portray people and situations that it has such a powerful effect.

Ivan Barac, *Hrvatska književnost*, vol.1, Zagreb 1964

Note on the Croatian Edition of 1992

This year marks the 150th anniversary of the first edition of *A Glance into Ottoman Bosnia* (1842). The present edition follows the design of the second, edited by Slavko Ježić and published in 1938, which differed only minimally from the first imprint. As is true of Ježić's edition, this one too retains the picturesque language and grammar of the original.

Milan Šarac, Zagreb 1992